FOOTBALL IS A NUMBERS GAME

Library of Congress Cataloging-in-Publication Data

Names: Coller, Matthew, author.
Title: Football is a numbers game : Pro Football Focus and how a
   data-driven approach shook up the sport / Matthew Coller.
Description: Chicago, IL : Triumph Books, [2023] |
Identifiers: LCCN 2023019610 | ISBN 9781637272183 (hardback)
Subjects: LCSH: National Football League—Statistics. |
   Football—Statistical methods. | Pro Football Focus (Organization) |
   BISAC: SPORTS & RECREATION / Football | SPORTS &
   RECREATION / General
Classification: LCC GV955.5.N35 C647 2023 | DDC
   796.33202/1—dc23/eng/20230515
LC record available at https://lccn.loc.gov/2023019610

This book is available in quantity at special discounts for your group or organization. For further information, contact:
   Triumph Books LLC
   814 North Franklin Street
   Chicago, Illinois 60610
   (312) 337-0747
   www.triumphbooks.com

Printed in U.S.A.
ISBN: 978-1-63727-218-3
Design by Nord Compo
Photos courtesy of the author unless otherwise indicated
Illustrations by Jake Kelly

FOOTBALL IS A NUMBERS GAME

Pro Football Focus and How a Data-Driven Approach Shook Up the Sport

MATTHEW COLLER

TRIUMPH
BOOKS

CONTENTS

FOREWORD

OOTBALL HAS GOTTEN SMARTER over the last decade. *Everyone* inside the sport is armed with more information than they were a decade ago, and the vast majority of the smartest people—coaches, fans, media members, players—use it. The best teams build departments around it, acquire players based on it, and call plays with it in mind. This has not always been the case. However slowly you think the football world has moved over the past 100 years, it moved slower than that. If you talked to some of the few analytics departments in place even 10 years ago, you'd hear how hard it was for them to get a meeting with a position coach to go through even the most basic of concepts.

Football over the last decade has been defined by a sort of information war, an arms race to not only mine the sport for data but learn how to use it. It's only been in this timeframe that the general public could get access to all-22 footage to fully quantify scheme or player movement. Or use player tracking data on pads to build models on how teams and players operate. The near-instant availability of film at every level has produced a football world where it is easier to see a play on a Friday or Saturday at a lower level and steal it the next week—and distribute it to your team via iPad. Football is a beautiful game; it is a violent game; but it is also an intellectual game, and never has that last part been as important as new ideas enter the sport on a near-weekly basis.

New ideas clash with old ideas every week in NFL facilities, and marrying the two is the only way forward. Football is a game of tiny little edges adding up to big ones, and there have never been so many opportunities to get those edges.

When Matthew Coller told me he was writing this book, I was immediately impressed; you cannot tell the story of football in the last decade without Pro Football Focus. Even if there are coaches or fans who *want* to, it's simply not possible—every team has a subscription and utilizes the data. Every network uses it to research players and schemes. It is not the only place to look for NFL information, but the point of football is there will *never* be one place to look. It is a ludicrously complicated sport, and that's the beauty of it. There's never one thing to look at on a play; there are probably *thousands* of factors to consider, and PFF helps simplify that conversation. Analytics have made the game more accessible and digestible—if you want to quickly see how many pass-rush snaps Micah Parsons had last year, you can find out in about 90 seconds. If you love studying football and you are over the age of about 30, you remember when you had it bad. *Really, really bad.* It means you searched the internet, often to no avail, for information as simple as player snap counts or for some grainy all-22 footage that was, at best, a copy of a copy. We get all of it now.

The football conversation has moved forward in the last decade. This is inarguable—analysts like Mina Kimes, Bill Barnwell, Ben Solak, and Steven Ruiz, among many others, make me smarter on a weekly basis, and the fact there are numbers to marry with the film when talking about the sport is a *huge* part of it. At PFF, folks like Seth Galina, Steve Palazzolo, or Sam Monson are some of my first reads of the week. Other football analytics pioneers like Football Outsiders are right alongside them. Every team now has an analytics department, and if you think the media and services like PFF didn't help normalize this, you are nuts.

Football is pushing forward. Even if, for many years, it didn't want to. I sometimes think of a line in a 2012 piece about Pro Football Focus that my then colleague Reed Albergotti wrote, before most people knew of the site. The Giants, who were about to win their second Super Bowl in four years on the weekend the story ran, utilized the website to scout opponents, and the story describes the process in which PFF founder Neil Hornsby and the Giants head of football information talk: "These communications typically begin with an email to Mr. Hornsby asking him to call Giants headquarters. That is because the team's low-cost telephone system won't allow calls to England."

This is the tension in the modern game: NFL teams are worth billions of dollars but have not typically embraced spending money on technology or emphasizing anything new at all. ESPN's Seth Wickersham once quoted an executive calling NFL franchises "billion-dollar lemonade stands."

The last decade has meant at least installing a laptop in that lemonade stand. For the best teams, it means building a franchise around the idea that new edges are out there, and you have to go get them. That's modern football.

Kevin Clark, senior football writer, The Ringer
April 2023

INTRODUCTION

A S SOON AS LEGENDARY NFL writer Peter King walked out of the Philadelphia Eagles' practice facility, he pulled out his phone and called Neil Hornsby. He couldn't wait to tell Neil about the 90-minute conversation he'd just had with Eagles head coach Doug Pederson, offensive coordinator Frank Reich, and receivers coach Mike Groh.

A week earlier, the Eagles had won the Super Bowl at U.S. Bank Stadium in Minneapolis. After they beat the New England Patriots 41–33, Reich made a comment to King that he wanted to share the story of the game-winning touchdown. So at 9 AM on the Saturday after Philly raised its first Lombardi Trophy, King and the Eagles coaches gathered at the NovaCare Complex in Philadelphia to break down quarterback Nick Foles' 11-yard pass to tight end Zach Ertz with 2:21 remaining in the fourth quarter, which put the Eagles ahead for good.

The coaches explained to King that they had put together a 194-play game plan for the Super Bowl, but Pederson still wasn't satisfied. Pederson asked all his coaches to pore over everything and look for any plays that might be better. When Groh arrived in Minneapolis, he spent Monday evening at the Radisson Blu Hotel at the Mall of America on the hunt for any possible weakness in the New England defense that they could exploit.

Using information from the football data company Pro Football Focus (PFF), Groh hunted through different types of plays that might give him any hints and discovered that the Patriots had struggled to cover formations that had three receivers together on one side and a tight end isolated on the other. The PFF system allowed Groh to pull up all the video clips of the Patriots defending those formations and find potential opportunities to create open receivers. One particular play that caught his attention was a 43-yard gain by the Carolina Panthers against the Patriots earlier in the season. Could they recreate the same type of play? Groh took his findings to Reich, and he agreed it was worth a shot. They went to Pederson, who loved the idea and agreed to put it in the game plan.

"Just like in basketball, right?" Groh told King for his Monday Morning Quarterback column for *Sports Illustrated* in February 2018. "When you isolate and put everybody on one side of the court and you send Kobe over to go do what he does. Same principle. We knew that they were going to overplay the bunch."

The Eagles used a unique wrinkle that they called "star motion," in which the running back rotates behind the quarterback before the snap. That gave Foles a hint about what type of defense the Patriots were playing based on how their players moved in response. On the other sideline, the Patriots coaches had an inkling that the ball might be going to Ertz. NFL Films' recap captured them calling for a double team, but the motion threw off the defenders.

In designing the formation, the Eagles put the three receivers bunched together because it created a "legal pick." In case Ertz wasn't open, Foles would have other choices. They had been studying bunch formations and using the PFF data to study teams that had used them successfully all season.

"One of the things we asked Mike at the beginning of the year was always look at stacks and bunches," Reich told King. "We always feel like stacks and bunches are important to understand how things play out. He is our stacks and bunches guru. We use PFF to give us a folder of stacks and bunches every week."

Though the Eagles used the concept only a handful of times during the regular season, the coaching staff made it play No. 145 on Foles' wristband. And then Pederson called for No. 145 in the biggest moment in franchise history. Coincidentally, the owner of PFF, Cris Collinsworth, was on the broadcast for NBC and pointed out before the snap that Ertz had a one-on-one matchup. Foles and Ertz executed the play. Philly became Titletown.

When Neil answered the phone, King told him, "You won't believe this: the Eagles used Pro Football Focus to help win the Super Bowl."

Neil was on his way to dinner with his wife, Claire. When he heard the Eagles were willing to tell the story of how PFF helped them and that one of his biggest supporters was going to write it, he got choked up.

"He was in awe," King said over the phone. "In a span of 10 years PFF went from the unwanted stepchild to the most valuable person at the table. I just thought, 'I'll be happy when a lot of people read this.' The people who say that Pro Football Focus is joke science, I'll be happy when they read that the Philadelphia Eagles used it in part to win the most important game in franchise history. That's what went through my mind."

In a football universe where every centimeter is covered, most people have never heard of Neil Hornsby.

There are a lot of potential explanations for why one of the most influential figures of the last 20 years in the NFL is relatively unknown to people outside of NFL front offices and the walls of PFF's Cincinnati home base. It might be because there were so many skeptics within the football world in the early days of PFF that most have begrudgingly accepted its place in the game but aren't interested in celebrating the company or its founder. It might be because Neil's background is in business, not football. He isn't exactly an "analytics guy" himself. He doesn't publish endless articles with spreadsheets galore. He isn't big on social media and doesn't give lectures about his own influence on the game of football.

Neil Hornsby built Pro Football Focus by putting together a team of several die-hard football fans, one tech genius, and a couple math wizards who made his passion come to life. He never dreamed that the teams he once read about in a magazine and dialed into Armed Forces Radio to hear play in the UK would be using his company's statistics to shape their organizations. He never dreamed he would end up running the company with an NFL legend. He never would have thought he would someday be a multimillionaire because of it or that he would be responsible for making the dreams of dozens of other people like him come true with jobs inside the game they love.

What's stunning is how quickly it happened. In a little more than a decade, PFF went from a company that was run out of Neil's spare room to being omnipresent in football.

Pro Football Focus now has tentacles in every facet of the game, from shaping the way coaches game plan to building models that help teams better understand the draft to whittling down a player's exact worth to dollars and cents to influencing the way football fans across the globe understand the sport.

All 32 NFL teams and more than 120 college teams have contracts with PFF. Their numbers are used on nearly every football broadcast network, most outwardly *Sunday Night Football* on NBC, and the company was valued at $160 million during a recent investment purchase.

Yet somehow coverage of PFF's rise to prominence has been limited to a handful of articles, starting with the *Wall Street Journal* writing about the New York Giants using data from PFF prior to their 2011 Super Bowl victory over the New England Patriots. Several PFF employees have become well known to the public through content produced in the form of articles and podcasts, but the company has full-time employee numbers in the hundreds and total contributors in the thousands. The story of how it got here has essentially never been told.

That could be because the analytics movement in football has just begun.

The Eagles didn't just win the Super Bowl because PFF data pointed them toward a single play. Pederson also took the advice of the team's analytics department and began "risking it" on fourth down more often than expected. Studies have long shown that the benefits of getting a first down routinely outweigh the downside of a turnover on downs, but coaches were slow to adopt the more aggressive approach. In years before, you would have heard coaches say that fans were irrational for wanting them to take fourth-down chances. A common saying was, "If you start listening to fans, you'll be sitting with them."

In the Super Bowl, Pederson was unafraid of ending up with the fans. His squad had reached the Big Game despite losing quarterback Carson Wentz to injury late in the season. He knew that in order to beat the NFL's greatest quarterback, Tom Brady, he couldn't punt the ball away or settle for field goals. Just before halftime, the Eagles had a three-point lead and were set up with fourth-and-goal from the 1-yard line. Rather than take the field goal and head into the half up by six, Pederson called for a trick play that came to be known as the "Philly Special." Tight end

Trey Burton threw a touchdown to uncovered quarterback Nick Foles, putting the Eagles up by 10. They eventually won the game by eight.

There had been other instances of coaches going for fourth downs in the Super Bowl and plenty of other fourth-and-goal touchdowns scored, but Pederson's aggressiveness sent a shockwave through the league because it worked in such a glorious upset. Since then, fourth-down attempts have shot up, and signs are everywhere that data is beginning to drive decisions in the NFL.

In 2021, NFL teams statistically went for it on fourth downs rather than punting more than they ever have before. A decade prior, attempting a pass on fourth-and-5 at the opponent's 50-yard line early in a game would have only been seen in *Madden* video games. If a head coach punts the ball away now, boos will rain down and fans watching from their couches will furiously publish critical tweets. The league also increased its usage of pre-snap motion and play-action, two concepts that have been proven to increase yards per play. Beyond the actual game play, we see examples of data-driven decisions in front offices as well. Between 2008 and 2010, 11 running backs were selected in the first round of the NFL draft. Between 2019 and 2021, there were four (and discussions about moving one of them to wide receiver). Teams are aware that drafting running backs with high picks isn't statistically a very good value play.

These are versions of things we have seen in other sports. Baseball teams no longer sacrifice bunt. Basketball teams avoid mid-range jump shots at all costs. Everyone has accepted that those things are simply inefficient. These data-driven advances in sports are paired with sports science, health, psychology, and ideologies that are influenced by corporations when it comes to leadership and culture. Those inside pro sports front offices are constantly drinking out of a firehose of new information, which has caused a shift in the way that decision-makers are forced to think and communicate.

It's not so much that the use of statistics just began; rather, it's that the analytical mind-set of other, more data-focused sports reached football. It was not long ago that tiebreaks for important debates on roster moves or draft picks in the NFL were determined by who was willing to "stand on the table" for their player. If a trusted scout could make a passionate plea for his guy, that would routinely be enough to sell the front office or coaching staff on a decision. The scene in *Moneyball* in which a scout claims that a player's ugly girlfriend was at the heart of his opinion was probably an unfair characterization of scouting, but that is some version of how the shots were getting called. Scouting is still an incredibly valuable part of the process, but a player's skill set is now analyzed in context along with supporting data.

During a guest appearance on the *PFF Forecast* podcast, former Atlanta Falcons general manager Thomas Dimitroff explained the evolution of decision-making within NFL buildings in recent years.

"For so long there was always that feeling in those scouting rooms and with coaches in there with the scouts, it was whoever had the loudest voice at times," Dimitroff said. "Or maybe it wasn't the loudest voice, it was, 'I just feel it in my heart.' You can't pull that off anymore. There is no way…. When you have that many people who have been studying a draft class or a free agency class for months, there is no way they can just suggest because they watched a handful of games that they are going to say, 'I just feel it deep inside, there's something I feel about that.' To pull in all the [data]…that goes such a long way when you're trying to prove your point."

Dimitroff continued:

"As a former general manager sitting down with the head coach and his staff, it's so important to be able to have a strong foundation and strong evidence. Something beyond, 'Hey man, I've been coaching this position for 25 years, I know this kind of linebacker.' That no longer carries its weight...to be able to have those conversations with strong evidence backing your opinion goes so much further in dissuading or persuading people on a coaching staff, your owner, or whoever may be opponents to a point you're trying to prove. It's so much more effective to do it that way."

Football's transformation doesn't have a "big bang" moment like Beane's Oakland A's emerging from the basement to contention on a limited budget. It doesn't have the Golden State Warriors breaking the NBA single season wins record while gunning threes from all corners of the arena. It has been a more deliberate change that has accelerated over the past 10 years with some landmarks along the way.

One such landmark was the instant success of college coach Chip Kelly's outside-the-box schemes. He took the skeptical NFL by surprise in 2013. Kelly had worked his way up in college football from coaching defensive backs and special teams at Columbia in 1990 to running the most exciting offense in college football (called the "blur" offense) at Oregon in 2012. He caught the eye of NFL teams because of his innovation and interest in searching every inch of the game for edges, whether that was running up-tempo or using formations that had never been attempted at the NFL level.

When he was hired by the Eagles, it was common to hear talk about how Kelly's college concepts wouldn't work in the NFL.

"It's going to be interesting to see if this style of offense projects to the NFL," legendary Eagles quarterback Ron Jaworski said, via Phillymag.com. "I'm going to say no."

"The NFL is a different league with fast players that have all week to prepare for you," Jaworski continued.

Pundits like Jaworski were wrong. Kelly turned the Eagles around from a 4–12 to 10–6 team in one season, and their scoring offense shot up from 29th in 2012 to fourth in 2013.

Kelly's tenure didn't last in Philadelphia, in part because the league copied everything his offenses did well and defenses adapted to stop the way he was running it. But his short time with the Eagles left a lasting impression on the way teams scheme offensively and the way commentators analyze outside-the-box thinkers.

While Pro Football Focus did not design Kelly's offense or directly tell Pederson to go for it on fourth down or convince the NFL world at large to follow the numbers, the data company that first emerged on the radar days before the 2012 Super Bowl has been center stage for the NFL's analytics explosion of the 2010s and early 2020s.

When I set out to tell PFF's story, I did not realize that Hornsby, who turned 57 in 2021, would end up walking away from PFF just as it was becoming a powerhouse beyond his wildest imagination. During our first meeting at his home in Cincinnati, he only hinted at the possibility of leaving his post as the chief executive officer in years to come. But in the year between my first and last meeting with Neil, the company underwent enormous change that sped up the process of its founder's departure.

The end of Hornsby's time at PFF was unceremonious. He exited after a six-month sabbatical that had been preceded by weeks of debate over the future of the company following a gigantic investment from a private equity firm called Silver Lake. There were simply things that he and chairman Cris Collinsworth could not agree upon. So, Hornsby went with a small party and a 700-word note to everyone in the company saying goodbye, and that was that. One of the most influential figures in football saw his departure covered in only one article, and that came in the *Cincinnati Business Courier*.

"Neil is the guy who gave birth to something that's unimaginable," Collinsworth told the *Courier*.

One year before the end of his tenure, Neil came to pick me up at the airport on a humid July day. I got into his Audi S7 and somewhere in between him complaining about American drivers and talking about the Minnesota Vikings' offseason, I asked him why he was letting a beat reporter from Minnesota tell his story instead of someone more well known or longer tenured covering football.

"Because you wanted to do it," he said.

That's the perfect summation of how Hornsby built one of the most successful sports data companies in the world: through a team of people who wanted to do it. So I decided the only way to tell the story of PFF is through the individual tales of the people who built it, the people whose lives have been changed by it, and the people who are tasked with taking it into the future. Their timelines make it impossible to stay in perfect chronological order, but the pieces will all come together along the way.

Chapter 1

THE DATABASE

N EIL HORNSBY fell in love with American football in 1983. He grew up a shy kid from a middle-class family in England, his father working in local government and his mother in retail at a store chain called Marks and Spencer. When he was 11 years old, he went off to grammar school. At his school, they told him that soccer, a game he grew up loving, was for riffraff. That was around the time of hooliganism and stadium disasters. Soccer was painted as violent and played by the uncouth. Students played cricket or rugby, and if you couldn't do either of those you ran track. So Neil played cricket and never developed the love for soccer that many of his countrymen share.

In Neil's youth there were only three channels in the UK, BBC-1, BBC-2, and ITV, so his access to broadcast sports was limited. On Saturdays, ITV would run horse racing, wrestling, and sports updates. Every so often they would toss in the odd sport to fill some extra space. That included a 15-minute highlight recap of the Super Bowl. That was Neil's only consumption of football until 1983, when a fourth channel launched.

The launch of Channel 4 changed everything. The new station ran National Football League games from the previous week at 6 p.m. every Sunday, and it quickly became appointment viewing

Neil Hornsby set out to better quantify events on a football field for his own entertainment and ended up building a company used by all 32 NFL teams.

for Neil. The first game he watched was an epic battle between Joe Montana's San Francisco 49ers and the Dan Marino–led Miami Dolphins. Well, it wasn't exactly the entire game. It was a chopped-down one-hour recap that focused on the best game of the week. Still, he wanted to see more Marino. In need of more football, Neil started tuning into games on Armed Forces Radio so he could paint the entire picture of a game inside of his head rather than only getting a summation of the best plays that happened the week before.

"Sometimes it would be perfect and then it would fade in and fade out and it would go something like, 'And it's third-and-12 and Marino drops back to pass and *shhhhhhhhhhh*,'" Neil said in his

British accent, which has remained strong after eight years in the United States. "Super frustrating. But I think just how much I loved football was evident based on how much I was willing to put up with just to listen to the games. You would listen to two games for six hours of substandard radio where at times you couldn't tell what was going on. It was just probably indicative of how much I love football."

One day when Neil was coming home from University in Liverpool, he ran across something at a train station that changed his life—*Touchdown* magazine. Dan Marino was on the cover. Neil started reading on the train and was hooked. *Touchdown* didn't just have articles about Marino and players about whom Neil had only a vague understanding from TV and radio; it had statistics on top of statistics for every team.

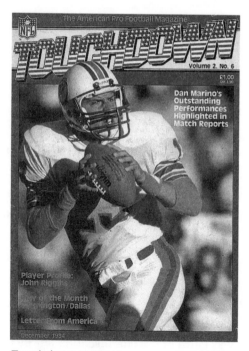

Touchdown magazine was a rare NFL publication in England. It got Neil Hornsby hooked on football.

Neil is telling the story of his early football fandom while sitting on his back patio that overlooks his kidney-shaped pool and gazebo. A grin comes across his face as he talks about *Touchdown*. Neil jumps up, walks inside, and then comes out a few minutes later with several magazines in his hands.

"That's the exact one that I bought at Lime Street Station," he says. "I read every single one of these. All of these little things here. Now when I look at box scores, they are boring and not relevant at all, but back in the day box scores were everything to me. Everything."

Neil pulls another magazine off his shelves, *Don Heinrich's Pro Preview '90*, starts flipping through the pages, and begins reading a report. "This guy is one of the best pulling guards in the league," the magazine asserted.

Neil stops. Looks up from the magazine, lifts up his sunglasses, and says, "How can they know that? In order to say that you have to have watched every player and put some form of metric in place to determine that and then determine how he performs in pull blocks in the running game and then measure him against every other player."

This is the essence of Neil Hornsby. Pro Football Focus' founder is both obsessive and curious. His personality is such that he wakes up before 5 AM to work out and eats the same breakfast every day. At the same time, he constantly questions conventional thinking. If you make a statement to Neil, you will need a sound argument and likely an internet connection to fact check. During my visit to Cincinnati, we walked around downtown and debated a player's trade value for six blocks.

He's also fascinated by leadership. Neil went to college for physics because he was good at it in high school, but he couldn't hang with the college-level courses. Instead, he found his true niche in the cricket club as the "social secretary," which we would probably call an event planner. He wasn't all that good at thermodynamics and wasn't a particularly great cricket player, but he discovered his real talent was planning and leading the group.

"I knew I was pretty good at organizing people," Hornsby said. "Taking command and saying, 'This is the plan, this is what we're going to do, guys.' Not being a dickhead but saying, 'This is the plan, what do you think about this?' Getting everybody on board. I was quite good at that."

Neil's first job out of college was working at a department store called BHS. He got into an apprenticeship program that allowed him to spend time in different areas of the store. From finance to logistics to human resources, he got to see how it all worked.

Neil had a manager at the BHS training store named Keith Smalls, whom he came to deeply respect. He remembered other managers from the chain being brought to their store to see how Keith had organized his Christmas display. Neil was on the hunt for an item when he overheard some of the other managers complaining and talking about how their stores were just as good, even if they weren't close. Neil went to Keith and asked why he was so much better than the other managers.

"Neil, I'm not particularly good; they're just a bunch of lazy wankers," Keith told him.

The idea that effort was most of the battle stuck with Neil.

He unexpectedly quotes the influential 1600s French nun Angelique Arnauld: "Perfection exists not in doing extraordinary things but in doing ordinary things extraordinarily well."

Neil gets back to reading more *Heinrich's Pro Preview*.

"'Perry is still learning pass blocking techniques and the proper angles,'" he reads aloud, then pauses for a moment. "Sounds OK in principle. What's the chance of it being accurate?"

In the late '80s, the obsessive part of Neil's brain was firing on all cylinders in regard to football. He needed to find a way to interact with the NFL beyond listening, watching, and reading *Heinrich's Pro Preview*. So he sold his comics collection to buy a personal computer. He got a Lotus 1-2-3 with a green-and-white screen and started building a football database. Hornsby started gathering football almanacs with all the league's games and statistics inside them and plugging the information into his PC.

In the early days, creating a football database was an escape from a failing marriage. Neil got married in 1988 and had two kids while he was still in his twenties. Two years later he started the database and by 1997, he was divorced. When Neil tells me that his ex-wife didn't love him, it feels as sharp as a paper cut, but he says it in a self-critical way—he pushed her to marry him when she didn't feel the same way about him as he did about her.

"It's just difficult and I think there was an air of resentment that built up and our marriage became quite a difficult one," Neil said. "I think like a lot of people with difficult marriages, my response to that was to work harder and I took myself away on a football database."

When Pro Football Focus started to emerge on the scene in the early 2010s, Neil was a mysterious figure because he wasn't a known journalist or former player. As his data started to pop up, so did rumors about his background. One in particular stuck out to him: that he was a wealthy fellow who was fiddling around with American football as a way to spend his riches.

Neil was the farthest thing from rich in the database days. When he got divorced, he sold his computer and put the database on hold. He took out a $30,000 loan to pay off credit cards and began shopping on a shoestring budget so he could support his ex-wife and two kids along with his own one-bedroom apartment, which he describes as being in "the shittiest part of Luton." When the boys would visit, they slept in his bed and he slept on the floor. Their visits were the only time he didn't eat something out of a can.

Neil met Claire in 1998 while working at the hospitality company Whitbread. It wasn't long after that when she bought him a new PC and he got back to working on the database, sometimes for as long as eight hours a day.

Claire's part in Neil's success is not small. Her patience for his football obsession stretched to the ends of the earth, even when there were times he would rather stay home for an entire day typing in numbers than spend time with her.

"I remember Claire sitting me down, she said, 'Neil, you have two choices in this: you can either sit here and do your database and do all of the various bits and pieces associated with it and that's fine, me and the kids will go down into town and we'll have a good time and we'll come back and know you love us and that's fine, or, alternatively, you can come with us and enjoy yourself and have a good time.' She said, 'I don't mind either of those two things, you need to make a choice,'" Neil said.

He is well aware that most life partners would not take this approach. He remembers distinctly one day when he was plugging numbers into the computer as usual and Claire asked if he was going to come outside to play with the kids. He gave her the standard line that it would only be 10 more minutes and before she walked away, Claire stood by the door and said, "Just tell me this is all going to be worthwhile."

"I can't," he responded.

At that time Neil didn't really even understand why he was doing the database. When I asked him why he kept going with it, he had several different answers: he wanted to publish it on the internet and use it to find people who could have conversations with him about football. He wanted to finish what he started. It was a habit that he'd had for so long, it was part of his life. Probably a combination of all three.

But when Claire wondered aloud if the hours spent were going to be worth it, there was nothing tangible he could show to prove that it would be. He never thought that he would make beer money off football data, much less millions.

"That really almost destroyed me," he said. "This is a person you love more than anything else in the world asking you whether something you're doing that you think deep down has no fundamental value to anybody else other than you, whether you should continue it or whether this is going to be worthwhile. But what do obsessive people do? They put that to the back of their mind. They think about it for a while and carry on anyway."

Claire remembers that comment differently. She recalled saying it when Pro Football Focus was getting closer to becoming a real company and she meant it with much more hope than scrutiny. If you were a betting man, you'd guess it was probably said more than once along the way and with different meanings to both of them.

By 2003, Neil wanted to publish the database on the internet. The greatest feeling in the world for Neil is when he finishes something that he has set out to do. You should see him buzzing around in the morning when he completes a workout. So you can imagine how excited he was to finally create the ultimate archive of NFL history. Then it came crashing down in one moment.

Neil was poking around the internet for something related to the database and he landed on Pro Football Reference. For the uninitiated, Pro Football Reference is, well, the ultimate archive of NFL history. Someone had beaten him to it.

Neil stood shellshocked.

"I remember it was probably one of the worst days of my life," he said. "I just knew that it was 13 years of effort down the toilet. I can remember standing in the shower and feeling completely despondent. What on earth have you done? Why on earth did you spend all of this time? Why on earth did you do all of this stuff?"

That's the point where most stories end. He probably should have given up on the idea and gone back to watching football as a regular fan. But it was the curious side of Neil's personality that kept pushing him forward with his project. He thought, *How can I make something different from Pro Football Reference?*

He was reminded of *Touchdown* magazine and some of the bullshit about left guards being good at pulling. As he'd gone along as a curious football lover, he discovered *Sports Illustrated's* famed Dr. Z, whose real name was Paul Zimmerman. What Neil loved about Dr. Z was that he backed up his opinions with empirical evidence. Zimmerman would tape games and watch them back closely, with a scoring system for each player. Oftentimes his opinions would stray from the mainstream when it came to writing about player awards, which Neil respected.

"He was different in so many different areas and he would write and justify exactly why he was going with such and such over such and such," Neil said. "There was a real power to me in saying, 'I've done this, this is the methodology I've used, this is the reason I've come to this conclusion, you can disagree with whatever you want but there's a methodology there.' Therefore, you could go back and he said he played well in these games and graded him as such and such. Could you do that with any of this bullshit?" Neil asked, pointing to the *Heinrich's Pro Preview* magazine on the table.

Neil read Dr. Z's book *The Thinking Man's Guide to Pro Football* over and over and couldn't get enough of Zimmerman's flair for analysis. Maybe there was something he could do that would produce more insight than the box scores?

At the same time Neil was licking his database wounds and brainstorming the next idea, something significant happened in the sports world: England won the World Cup in Rugby.

This was the first time in Neil's life that a team he was follow-ing won a championship. His beloved Miami Dolphins, unfor-tunately, came up short when they had a chance against the San Francisco 49ers in January 1985. England's victory came down to a final kick, and Neil went berserk with joy. Amidst the cel-ebration, he wanted to read everything and anything he could get his hands on about that magical club, and he came across an interesting story.

One of the players on the team, Will Greenwood, wrote an autobiography, and in it he told an anecdote about how he would evaluate his own performances. Greenwood noticed that sometimes he would feel good about the way he played but the media and fans would not celebrate his game at all. They would, however, heap praise upon him when he scored, even if the rest of the contest wasn't up to par. The most accurate feedback, Greenwood wrote, actually came from his dad, who created a grading system for judging his son's game that they would go over afterward.

This idea clicked with Neil. The only way to figure out if some-one was the best pulling guard in the league would be to watch every game, mark down what that guard did on each play, and compare it to the other guards.

But how would he watch the full games in order to create such a grading system for football? Well, timing was on Neil's side. A company called Pontel, which sold VHS tapes and DVDs, had just started making every NFL game available for sale. If a game was played on Sunday, Neil could have the DVD of that game in his mailbox by Wednesday or Thursday. So he drew up spreadsheets in pencil and started marking down things about each play and then plugging it into a new database.

It didn't have a name yet, but Pro Football Focus was born.

An example of Neil Hornsby's earliest tracking of NFL data by hand with pencil and paper.

Chapter 2

PFF IS BORN

IN 2005, WHEN NEIL HORNSBY was just starting to formulate his grading system, he was working as a commercial director for a restaurant chain called Little Chef and doing work for the parent company Travelodge. His boss at Travelodge called one day and said he wanted to see Neil in the office at 6 AM the following day. The office was an hour away, so that meant getting up and out of the house for this meeting before five. *This must be some kind of important meeting,* Neil figured.

When Neil arrived, his boss said, "I have good news and I have bad news."

Bad news first, Neil requested.

"You're fired."

"Bloody hell, what is the good news then?" Neil responded.

"We're taking you on as a contractor and we're giving you more money."

What an unnecessary way to tell someone they're getting a raise.

Travelodge was massaging the books, apparently dressing up the company to sell it, and that involved categorizing Neil's job differently. So Neil started his own company as a contractor. The way it worked thereafter was that Neil would pay himself a salary and pay subcontractors to do management jobs, and he would end up with 10 to 15 percent of the revenue that came in on top of the salary. That meant doing quite a bit better financially.

"I'd take the amount of money that I was earning from subcontractors and throw it at the football stuff," Neil said. "I built this database, and I was getting into a situation where I was thinking, 'How can I up this game now?'"

Upping the game meant getting some help. It meant finding Employee No. 1: Ian Perks.

When Perks graduated from University of Leeds with a degree in information systems, he got a job as part of a graduate program working for a company called CSC, which, broadly defined, does "business solutions" for thousands of companies. He was assigned at first to work in information technology with British Aerospace and then around a year later he found another position working for a technical services company in Cambridge. That's where he met Neil Hornsby. In 2001, Neil had been brought in to manage a group

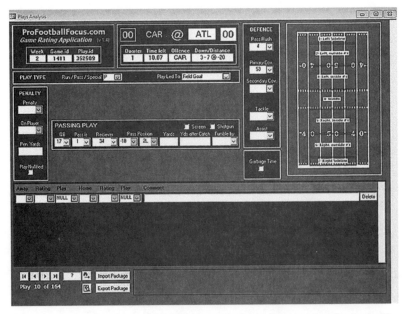

One of the earliest data collecting tools that Neil and Ian Perks built.

of people for the technical services and Perks worked as a program analyst, a position that was a few rungs down the ladder from Neil's.

About a year later, Neil left and didn't have any more contact with Perks. Initially, they had barely known each other, but they had a mutual friend named Ed McDermott who knew about Neil's obsession with American football and his database. Ed told Neil that if he needed someone to build a system to store his data, he should talk to Ian Perks. Coincidentally, Perks had just taken a new job at a small company and moved within a few miles of Neil's house. Perks agreed to come by. He wasn't particularly happy with his new gig and was looking for ways to build up his portfolio.

While Perks couldn't care less about American football, he loved the challenge that Neil presented. Growing up, Perks was enamored with computer games. In his early teens he would get magazines that had printed programs which needed to be copied verbatim into the BBC microcomputer. If they weren't typed in perfectly, they didn't work, so he typed them in perfectly. As he got older, he thought it would make for a good career, especially since he is colorblind and didn't qualify for a subset of paths that many people take, like policing or becoming an electrician. What really drew Perks to computer programming was the puzzles. There was always a new problem to be solved and he loved the chase of solving the riddles that computers presented. It was a trait he inherited from his dad, and it made him perfect for working on Neil's database.

Coming out of college, Perks had wanted to be a database analyst, so he saw Neil's project as a chance to do what he enjoyed most. For the first nine months or so, Neil was able to pay Perks to build his database, but expenses started piling up and Neil could no longer afford to do so. Instead, Neil used his contacts from his management experience to get Perks jobs that allowed him to leave the small company he'd been working for and become a freelance IT expert and for Ian to continue building the database on a more ad-hoc basis. They also became friends. Perks would come over to Neil's house once every week or so and get feedback on what he'd been building. He remembered Neil carrying his two young kids around the house before they'd get into the car and travel to Liverpool for their regular jobs.

"I'd drive up to his house and show him what I'd done, and he would say it was right or it was wrong or that he wanted some changes to it or he had some more thoughts about it," Perks said via Zoom from the UK. "It was early-stage development. He had a good idea of what he wanted, then I would go away and come back and ask, 'Is this what you meant?' That's how it built up."

When Neil asked Perks to start putting his database on the internet, it created a new problem to solve. Ian had never worked with web development before.

"That was a huge learning curve," Perks said.

As Neil brought on more people to add to the data they were collecting, Perks had to create a chain by which files could be loaded into his data collection tool and then shared in a ZIP file. They would create Excel spreadsheets that could be shared. The more people that came on board, the more they leaned on Perks to create more systems and build more tools to automate the processes. He loved it.

"I used to try to get a work-life balance, but I ended up drinking a bottle of red wine in the evening and coding until 1 or 2 in the morning," Perks said. "The time just passes because you enjoy the battle of the problem that's in front of you."

He noticed that coding for 12 to 14 hours per day between building PFF's data collection tools and website and his freelance contract jobs sharpened his programming skills. He was hired for a job working with a system that he'd never used before and quickly mastered it to the point that the company didn't need the other developers they had brought in. He could look at 100 lines of code and spot a single error within 30 seconds. He could work with five different people and know by their code which person had written a particular program. It was his superpower.

"It's quite artistic," Perks said.

A few years after Perks began helping Neil as a favor, the company was growing and forming relationships with teams. Neil needed something he could use while visiting teams that he could quickly print out and leave with them. In about six weeks, Perks and Neil cooked up what they called the Scouting Tool, which pulled in all types of data to publish a 40-page report into a PDF. The tool instantly provided them with team tendencies and relevant performance metrics that could help a team analyze an opponent or itself by the numbers. In 2023, an updated version is still being used routinely by teams.

"You set parameters—are you doing a self-scout or an opposition scout, what games do you want to pick, what sections of the report do you want—and it will build a PDF," Perks said.

Neil had sought to create a demonstration of what teams could do with the data by putting himself in their shoes. What would a coach want to know about themselves and their opponent?

"We built it only as a demonstration of the power of the data, but remarkably, it was a huge hit, and they used it pretty much as Ian and I wrote it," Hornsby said. "I was completely bemused."

About 10 years after it was put together in Excel, PFF moved everything to a new database, and it had to be recoded. Neil says it was one of his favorite moments that his son Ben, who is a junior software developer at PFF, was the person who recoded his invention so teams could keep using it.

Until 2014, Pro Football Focus was just a coding joyride for Perks. That's when he was asked to come on full time and move to Cincinnati. He had a young family and his wife, Allison, told him it was now or never because as his kids got older it would be harder to uproot them. He had done work in New Zealand and Australia before and thought it might be interesting to take a leap of faith. His wife and Neil persuaded him to come to the U.S. as the chief technology officer at PFF. They arrived in 2016.

As the company grew, the needs for more data tools grew, which meant hiring more people. Perks' team started off small and then increased to 12, and by 2018 he was managing 20 employees. The opportunities to do what he liked best—sitting up late at night writing code—more or less disappeared. Ian guessed that only about 15 percent of his time was being spent on his favorite part of the job by that point.

"You spend all your time managing and you don't end up doing the thing that you love to do anymore regardless of how much you'd like to do it," Perks said. "That's certainly been the challenge for me."

In 2018, he decided to return to the UK. He would have needed to get a green card and didn't want the company to spend the money on one if he wasn't sold on staying in Cincinnati. His mother was struggling from early onset dementia, and he wanted to get his life back. Being a workaholic has its benefits, but he realized that he had missed a lot. Perks remembered holding his third child in the hospital when his phone rang. It was Neil asking about an issue with the server. Going to work at 7 AM and leaving at 8 PM and then being ready to take on any other issues in the off hours wore him down.

He's still part of the company now, but not in the same way as before. He told Neil that he would continue helping out until they replaced him as CTO.

Perks' story represents a common theme at PFF. The original members who worked endlessly and joyfully to build the company later faced difficulties finding comfort in their roles as the company grew and changed.

Not that he has many regrets.

"I look back on it all very fondly," Perks said. "It was hard; it is not easy doing all that stuff. I think the experience is going to stand me in good stead whatever I decide to do. I'm pleased that I did it and that I took the step and the leap. Met some great people out of it and it's been a bit of a ride."

At the 2021 NFL Combine, which will likely be his last, Perks noticed the company had grown so much that when PFF had its get-together in the basement in the famed St. Elmo basement, people were asking what he did for the company.

"I was Employee No. 1," he said, laughing.

Ben Stockwell came along around the same time as Perks—call him Employee No. 1A or 1B—but took a very different path. He met Neil on an NFL UK message board. They exchanged messages and Neil told Stockwell about his concept of scoring each player on every play from a range of minus-2 to plus-2, which is the outline of how everything is still done in 2022.

He explained to Stockwell that it worked like this: if a quarterback makes one of the best throws of the year, that would get a plus-2. If he tosses the ball directly to a defender for an interception, that would be a minus-2. If the QB throws a screen pass, that's a zero because it's neither exceptional nor poor. An above-average throw into traffic would be a plus-0.5 and a simple overthrow is likely a minus-0.5. Now apply that logic to all the positions.

Stockwell was into it. The idea that a football-loving fella or two could grade 70 plays by every player in every game was absurd on its face, but Stockwell was in college and couldn't come up with any reason not to have a look at Neil's player grading concept, so he started doing grading while working toward a degree in ecology.

Stockwell got to work collecting all the scenarios for every position and how to appropriately grade the plays. What happens if a safety bites on a pump fake and gives up a wide-open touchdown pass? What happens if a receiver falls down and a pass is picked off? What happens if a defensive end gets a sack, but the defensive tackle caused the pressure? Everything was trial and error.

When Stockwell graduated from college, Neil asked, "Have you got a job yet?" He did not, so Neil offered to pay him to grade.

"It took me a few days to say yes to that because I was like, 'There has to be a catch here; no one is just going to pay me to watch American football,' but there wasn't a catch," Stockwell said over a Zoom call from his office in England.

Stockwell became an American football fan the same way Neil did: Channel 4. He explained that the NFL had waves of popularity in the UK. Neil had grabbed on the first time around in the '80s. Stockwell got onboard with the second wave in the '90s. He couldn't get enough of the video game *Madden 96* for PlayStation 1 and recalled watching the Packers–Patriots Super Bowl in 1997 as his first game. Much like in Neil's day—only a little more refined—Channel 4 would air a highlight show on Saturdays recapping the previous week's games. It was appointment viewing, even if the only live game he could take in at the time was the Super Bowl.

When Stockwell began working for Neil, he had absolutely no idea what he would do for a career after college. Most entry-level jobs in ecology require experience. How can someone gain enough experience to be qualified for a job if nobody will give them a job in the first place? He landed a part-time lab gig "chopping up bits of people's intestines" for health studies but didn't gain much traction in that field. Stockwell figured that giving Neil's football project a chance might pay off—and if it didn't, what harm was there in having given it a shot?

Shortly after bringing Stockwell aboard, Ian Perks built the PFF website so they could have a place to start housing his numbers. That's when the operation began gaining momentum.

"There was nothing that felt better than when you've done the process—there was a real hit to it—when you'd spent 16 hours doing a game, done it all, you'd press a button and then…the game would populate into what we'd call PSV1 and, 'Oh, the grades are there!'" Neil said. "It was so exciting to see those goddamn grades. This was for no other reason than as a fan, you'd never seen anything like it before. How'd this guy do in this game? And we felt pretty good about what we were doing. At that time if nobody else saw it and nobody else cared, what did we care? It wasn't for them; it was for us."

When Stockwell first started grading, the process was painfully slow. By the time the 2008 season was starting, they had only done half the 2007 season. The 2008 season was the first complete year that they graded, and that was completed only a month before the 2009 opener. Things actually sped up when Stockwell broke his arm. Coincidentally, he was playing football and got hurt, which limited his ability to write out full descriptions of each play and explanations for why each player had been graded the way they were. He came up with codes that he could type with his good arm and suddenly everything started to happen quicker.

Even with Stockwell's newly developed shorthand, they knew that the delivery of the grades had to be faster and more graders needed to be involved in order to produce results in a more timely fashion. In 2009, Stockwell trained Sam Monson, another PFFer Neil found on the NFL UK message boards, on the system. Stockwell spent hours on Skype calls with Monson going over different situations and plays and making notes of all the ways in which they felt like those events should be scored. By writing it down and putting logic and consistency behind the grading, it could be much more than a couple football fans and their own personal made-up fun stats; it could have some credibility to share with others. The process could also be easily taught, thus creating the potential for growth.

Once Monson mastered the system, which was around 2010, he could start training more people. They brought on two more graders. Those graders started to train more graders, the team began to multiply, and the delivery speed with which the grades could end up on the Pro Football Focus website kept increasing. With every trial and error, the nuances of the system became more and more detailed.

"Probably the first five, six, seven years that we had it was an evolution of me and the rest of the graders seeing things and being like, 'We don't like this,' or, 'We need to fix that,'" Stockwell said.

By 2022, PFF had more than 75 graders, a 300-page handbook, and a detailed cross-checking system.

In the early years, graders would give any game a single pass off the TV copy and then produce results. Now one grader will give initial scores for a game from the All-22 coaches' film and then each area of that game will be cross-checked by a separate team of graders who focus on individual position groups. For example, former NFL quarterback Bruce Gradkowski cross-checks all the quarterback, receiving, and coverage grades.

Through the years the grading process has undergone endless changes and adaptations. In 2015, the grades got a big boost from former NFL coach Mike Shanahan. After the Super Bowl–winning coach was let go by Washington, he asked PFF if it would be interested in hiring a member of his staff named Bobby Slowik, who was named the San Francisco 49ers' passing game coordinator in 2022. Bobby joined and played a major role refining the grades through the eyes of a coach.

"The reassuring thing there is that [former players and coaches] have been able to say, 'Big picture, yeah, you're in the right area but let's work on this area, let's work on that area,'" Stockwell said. "It feeds into that constant evolution…if you think you know all the answers, you haven't asked the right questions yet."

Slowik was hired as the Texans' offensive coordinator in 2023.

The same year that Slowik came onboard, the grading system went against its toughest challenge: a five-touchdown game by Aaron Rodgers. Early in the 2015 season, the All-Pro Packers quarterback threw for 333 yards and five touchdowns with zero interceptions in a win over the Kansas City Chiefs. Despite the box-score dominance, he was given a negative grade by PFF's system, setting off a firestorm of fans and media ready to burn the PFF offices to the ground.

"Scott Van Pelt was trashing us on ESPN," longtime PFFer Steve Palazzolo remembered.

Stockwell wrote a piece that broke down Rodgers' touchdown passes, pointing out that three of them weren't particularly difficult throws. He noted a fumble in which Rodgers graded negatively and a bad pass that could have turned into a pick-six had the Chiefs defender simply caught the ball.

"For a long time, one of the biggest articles that we ever had on the site was Ben writing an article justifying that grade," Monson said.

The incident put the grading system on the map more than any other particular inflection point. Reporters started going to players and asking what they thought of their grades, and it became a hot-button issue in locker rooms. It was one of the first major chances PFF had to show off the value of its system: it could open up the box-score curtain and give audiences a more accurate depiction of what happened—and the graders could show the how and why. Being contrarian would also become a staple of PFF. Leaning on the results and going against the establishment has long been a feature of the analytics movement but at the time the grades were introduced to football fans, there weren't many contrarian opinions to be had outside of the gambling world and the football analytics site *Football Outsiders*.

In 2016, the grades took another big step forward. Legendary offensive line coach Paul Alexander did a video comparing his grades to PFF's system and only found a handful of areas in which he disagreed with a score they had given his player. They released his findings on social media, pushing hard back against skeptics of the system.

"That really helped internally and externally," Stockwell said. "Particularly it being from an offensive line coach. That's the dark arts; there has never been numbers on the offensive linemen before."

You will still hear NFL people say that they aren't interested in the grades. That's not exactly true. The league's relationship with the grades could be better characterized as complicated. While many coaches and executives have publicly rolled their eyes, people inside the NFL have also played a major role in sharpening the system along the way.

"Mainly now my involvement in teams is dealing with requests in terms of, 'Could you add this to the data collection?'" Stockwell said. "Have you considered this? Why is this collected in this way?' And then starting to get more involvement from coaches, particularly pass-rush coaches who use the data and will send us notes each week through the service team to say, 'Thought this could have been a pressure from our guys,' and dealing with those requests back and forth."

Players also send PFF feedback. Some are very helpful when it comes to things like grading complicated coverages. Others are not so helpful, such as when players contact PFF simply wanting better scores to go on their grading sheets.

"I have players who have stopped talking to me," Stockwell said, laughing.

Stockwell said that it's jarring to think about having a team of 75 graders and people involved with the NFL working on a system that was born from a message-board friendship over football. The team is now able to get every NFL grade out by Monday morning and hammer out grades for every FBS (NCAA Division I Football Bowl Subdivision) college game to boot. PFF is dipping its toes into FCS (NCAA Division I Football Championship Subdivision, the second-highest level of college play) and may someday set its sights on doing major high school games.

In the early years when Neil first brought on Stockwell and a few others, he was draining his newly boosted bank account to add more and more games to the database. He was in over his head with the costs of a project that wasn't making a dime.

"It becomes an addiction, and you start paying more money than you should do, and all of the sudden I realized…that I paid people in a month, just a month, $5,000," Neil said. "Now, $5,000 might not feel like a lot, but you multiply $5,000 by 12 and that's going out, and I've paid tax on this to pay it out because it's a hobby, it's not like it's tax deductible or anything like that. It became apparent to me that I couldn't continue for any long period of time."

Neil called a meeting. He had bad news for the crew: he wasn't going to be able to continue paying them at the same rate. He told them that if they needed the money, he could work it out but if they didn't, he could pay them in company shares. Those shares were worth nothing and Neil told everyone that they would most likely never be worth anything. He kept paying Stockwell and Monson, and the rest were happy enough with their shares. After all, they were doing it to get their hands on the data anyway.

In 2009, the goal became to do the entire season and finish the grades by the Friday after each weekend of games. Neil got up every morning before dawn to grade and put in full-time hours per week on top of his consulting business, which was funding his time-consuming hobby. They were able to pull it off and grade the whole year.

"We were absolutely on our last legs," Neil said. "We'd done 100-hour weeks, the guys with full-time jobs, and everybody had worked incredibly hard, but we'd achieved it."

When Neil says that they were only doing it for themselves, he's not kidding. In 2008, the PFF website was averaging eight to 10 visitors per day, and that included people from PFF. Neil estimates it was closer to zero.

Khaled Elsayed's first article for the PFF site was definitely not read by anybody. He wrote somewhere in the ballpark of 10,000 words on the Atlanta Falcons for the earliest version of ProFootballFocus.com and didn't care about the subsequent clicks. Simply having somewhere to publish his football musings got him excited. It also got him to say yes to working with Neil after balking initially.

Elsayed is another PFF Original whom Neil found on the NFL UK forum. He grew a passion for American football simply by wanting to watch any and every sport that was on television. His parents and wife would tell you that has never changed. He remembers several of the more serious NFL UK forum fans getting frustrated with the discussion in the areas open to everyone and breaking off into a private member group that included Neil, who was the oldest and considered the sage of their little online community. Apparently, Monson had to sneak in under a different name because he was considered too combative. That would actually play in their favor later.

When Neil asked for volunteers for his grading project, Elsayed felt like it had the potential to answer questions that they had been asking for a long time in the forums. In October 2008, Elsayed agreed to come along, but he quickly became impatient with the lack of structure and decided not to bother with the two-bit operation. Still, he kept Neil's strange project in the back of his mind. He was working for the department of working pensions helping people who were unemployed find work, but didn't have any real career direction and was looking for some sort of sign to point him in the right direction.

That came when his girlfriend broke up with him and he moved back in with his parents a few months after originally turning down Neil. A little down on his luck, Elsayed offered to get back onboard, particularly because Neil had installed more processes for tracking and grading by then. At first, it was a disaster.

"I was like, 'This is boring, I can't figure out the difference between Harry Douglas and Laurent Robinson, it's impossible, I'm not going to do this,'" Elsayed said over Zoom from the UK.

So, he quit again and did some traveling. But he kept getting drawn back in by curiosity. He made a deal with Neil that he would track games if he could write for the website.

Once he started getting articles published, Elsayed became nearly as obsessed with PFF as Neil. He fell in love with the grades. He started taking his eye off the ball during games and watching matchups, and he couldn't wait to see what the grades said about who won between a receiver and corner or a defensive tackle and guard. Every minute that he was away from his full-time job was spent grading games or writing. He charted 125 games in the first year and wrote 10 to 15 articles per week. When Neil brought in revenue for the first time, Elsayed left his job and started working for PFF full time.

Before Elsayed worked at his gig helping unemployed people, he was a recruiter for an investment bank who was tasked with finding software developers. He soon became PFF's recruiter. Elsayed started looking for other people to track and grade games. The process was simple: he put up a post on the website and tweeted it out and then waited for people to email about their interest.

"The first time I did it I remember being out with a mate having drinks and it was like, wow, look at all these people emailing me. I got like 120 people, and I couldn't believe it," Elsayed said.

Of course, 120 people quickly became 20 people who were seriously interested.

"A lot of people who want to work in football don't want to work hard in football," Elsayed said.

He would send all the applicants a game that had already been deemed 100 percent accurate, give them a deadline, and then compare the results among those who actually turned in the game grades. While accuracy was generally the most important thing, he was looking for something else: enthusiasm.

You can teach someone a process to be more accurate. You cannot teach them to care. Elsayed knew that he didn't have much money to give, so he was overly patient. If somebody applied past the deadline, the team took a look at them anyway. If someone was late with their first game, Elsayed accepted their excuse and gave them another chance. A lot of Elsayed's time was wasted because of his patience, but he noticed that the cream quickly rose to the top and they started finding effective trackers, some who would eventually play massive roles in the company's success.

Elsayed felt incredibly confident that PFF could go somewhere. In the early days, Neil, Stockwell, Monson, and Elsayed would get together at Neil's house for meetings about their approach to the future. During the first few meetups everyone was friendly and cordial, but as they went along everyone began to offer more unfiltered opinions.

"Everyone was brutally honest with each other and there was a lot of confrontation," Elsayed said.

Elsayed became as serious about PFF as Neil, which sometimes resulted in battles within the group over how they planned to take the next big steps with the company.

"Every mistake we made would linger with me like, *We have to be better,* and every time someone criticized us it hurt me to my core," Elsayed said. "How do we defend it? We need to reach out. We need to prove to them that they are wrong.

"I wasn't always the easiest person to be around because I was so demanding," Elsayed continued. "In hindsight maybe I could have enjoyed the journey a little bit more but at the same time I think it was probably integral that we had someone that was just obsessed."

"I didn't have a social life, I was like, 'We have to make this work.'"

But his seriousness and intense drive were exactly what PFF needed. Elsayed became Neil's No. 2 in command in the early days, acting as the engine that brought Neil's ideas to life by pushing himself and everyone underneath him as hard as he could to make it work.

Elsayed created a competitive environment where everyone would pick a tweet to send out to see which one would have the most engagement. They would study the numbers—once people started reading the website—and watch closely whose articles did the most clicks. He opened the door for anyone to write for that site that wanted to contribute. He was always looking for ways to allow others to show they were buying in.

As the company grew, Elsayed didn't write as much. He got frustrated with crazed reactions on social media. Because of that, he isn't as recognized on the outside these days as much as other PFF personalities. Instead, he handled a bunch of different roles, from overseeing content to the quality control of the grading to managing the transition to charting college football games—which added dozens of people to the roster—to overseeing the transition from an offline emailing system to an online system where trackers could upload data themselves.

Elsayed's ability to find people to chart and then manage growth in recruiting and handling of the data is hardly the sexiest story of PFF's growth, but without the effort to find the most energetic and accurate trackers and then keeping the process organized, there would be no PFF. He understood the value and pushed his group. One person described Elsayed as "an asshole during the season, but when the season was over he would ask how everyone was doing."

As PFF grew and power was spread out, Elsayed's role as Neil's engine wasn't quite the same. Neil missed him being the person who could band the team together to push their ideas to fruition no matter the obstacles.

"There was a time post-2014 where we missed his drive," Neil said.

Now PFF is trying to repeat Elsayed's success in another realm: soccer. PFF has begun grading soccer games and communicating with clubs about using the data. The competition is stiffer, and Elsayed is trying to strike a work-life balance now that he has a family, but the same principles will need to apply for his second act within PFF to work. Of course, the landscape is a little different this time. Expectations of workers are higher than they were originally, when PFF was only made of a few friends trying to grade games, versus now, being a behemoth. It's not as easy as simply looking for the most energetic people.

"It's really interesting and something we're trying to convince people now as we go into this soccer venture—if you put something into it, you will get something out," Elsayed said. "If you expect to be handed something or expect to immediately get paid well, your motivation probably isn't right. That was the lucky thing about the group of people that Neil collected—everyone wanted to build something good. They took ownership of it and felt responsible for it and it's hard to do that."

Chapter 3

THE NEW YORK GIANTS COME CALLING

WHEN NEIL RECEIVED an email from someone claiming to be with the New York Giants, he thought it was one of his guys playing a joke on him.

He woke up Claire and asked her if she thought it could possibly be real.

"I must have spent ages Googling everything and I'm thinking, 'This is a fairly sophisticated scam for one of my mates,'" Neil said. "It was an email from the New York Giants saying, 'We read the stuff on the website, really liked your information but can you tell us who you are and how you can get some more of it, and can you give us a call?' That was the other thing. Why are the New York Giants asking me to call them? Why don't they ask for my number and call me? They're the New York Giants."

Neil emailed back and discovered that it was indeed the Giants. Specifically, Jon Berger, the team's director of football information. Berger needed Neil to call them because the Giants' switchboard didn't allow international calls. Imagine.

Berger had found PFF's website in late September 2009, following a Giants Week 3 win over the Tampa Bay Buccaneers. He was poking around the internet and came across player usage numbers that did not exist anywhere else.

"It seemed bizarre to me that some independent website would have [player usage] totals," Berger said over the phone. "It wasn't on a play-to-play basis, it was how many snaps each guy played for the game, but I figured if they have that then they have to have it on a play basis."

Berger went to his own data and checked the Giants' usage numbers against PFF's and found that PFF's data was accurate.

"I said, 'I don't know where he got these from but that's pretty darn good," Berger said.

When they spoke on the phone, Berger was at a game in Kansas City. He told Neil that the team was interested in PFF's player participation information.

"[Neil] described their network of people and how they were scattered everywhere. We were stunned…and he was just so dedicated. It was almost startling," Berger said.

The Giants wanted to know who was on the field for every play so they could create film clips (called cut-ups) of opposing players they wanted to scout. They could certainly gather it themselves, but they would need to dedicate manpower. With the job of tracking usage outsourced, it became instantly more efficient.

"Our pro scouts had to grade players and if they're grading a linebacker when the guy played 34 percent of the snaps, they still had to watch every snap to see when he was on the field," Berger explained. "If we attached the play time data to the video files then we can make specific cut-ups, which at the time was pretty good."

For whatever reason, the NFL did not provide this data to teams on a weekly basis in those days. It was embargoed until the end of the season. Berger could never understand why the NFL wouldn't let everyone have the usage statistics if everyone was tracking it anyway. But the league competition committee's stubbornness on the issue opened the door for Neil and PFF.

"It saved us so much time and from there you could do all sorts of matchup stuff and different kinds of video just using the data," Berger said.

It wasn't long after that the NFL started making the official player participation data available during the season. Neil remembers being in a meeting with Jacksonville's Mike Perkins, who oversees the technology department, in which Perkins expressed frustration at the fact they had to pay an outside company for player participation. Perkins sent an email to the NFL. That caused the league to eventually make the data available.

Neil thought that the NFL giving teams the official player participation numbers from week to week could leave PFF out in the cold, but teams had gotten a sniff of what they could get done by using PFF's tracking. There was growing demand for more data that went well beyond player usage. By 2010, the Giants started asking for more PFF numbers.

"Coach [Tom Coughlin] would come up and say, 'Hey, can we do this?' and I'd run it by them and they would send me a report…and it really helped us in 2010," Berger said. "Then we got even more in 2011. It was lots of different data they were providing for us, and we were able to utilize the data. I thought it was a competitive edge back then."

In 2011, PFF provided the Giants with their own liaison named Tyson Langland. He was there to answer any of their data inquiries and run reports at their request. When the Giants reached the Super Bowl, they got Langland a ticket.

The only tricky part of integrating PFF's numbers was that coaches and scouts absolutely despised the fact that PFF was also grading their players. A coach would read in the media that so-and-so player graded this or that way and wouldn't be happy with the conclusion, or a scout would resent the idea that any "non-football" people were evaluating players. So, when Berger got the data reports from PFF, he would delete the grade columns.

"I'd have to talk them down and say, 'We're not really interested in that, we just want objective information,'" Berger said.

Over the years, PFF's data became so commonplace that Berger stopped having to give his PFF grade spiel to new coaches.

"They've changed the game and how they provided information that everybody uses and now everybody takes it for granted, it's just there," Berger said. "Everybody builds upon the information that they provide.... I love to see different teams now take it and run with it and do different things. There have been a couple teams now that have built their own PFF leg systems and hired their own guys to break down the games and that's very impressive. It's wild."

Berger takes great pleasure in how far the NFL has come with technology and data since he first joined the Giants in the mid-80s.

When he was in college as a computer science and applied mathematics major, Berger worked for the team during training camp doing odd tasks. Ballboy, security—you name it. He got to know the Giants coaching staff, and when the club bought its first computers, they brought him onboard to program them. He wrote programs to track game analysis and worked with then defensive coordinator Bill Belichick on self-scouting and opponent scouting programs. Throughout the late '80s, they added college scouting and continued building applications. In 2007, the team gave Berger an analytics title, though he never wanted the world to know what he was working on.

Berger left the Giants in 2021 to work in the league office as an officiating trainer. He left a legacy within the Giants organization as a behind-the-scenes key player for four Super Bowl–winning teams. At PFF, he's the guy that started it all and inspired Neil to sell PFF to teams. So, every year at the NFL combine, the PFF guys take Berger to dinner.

"Neil's contribution to the league is unreal," Berger said. "I'm trying to think of a better word. His contribution is incredible. He's revolutionized the way NFL teams use data, and it drives everything. Everything we do is built upon the data. It's changed the world. I started doing this in the '80s, and thinking about how data has changed and the things we're able to do now, we couldn't have dreamed of the things we're doing now."

The relationship between PFF and the Giants never would have materialized if the PFF player usage numbers hadn't been accurate. Neil understood that the grades would always have an element of subjectivity to them, but the other data that they were gathering had to be exact or it was meaningless.

"There are certain parts of your business that you're never 80-20," Neil said, referring to the theory of business that 80 percent of the benefits should come from 20 percent of the effort. "The bit we never 80-20ed was the data, because we just loved it."

Coincidentally, it wasn't the Giants who were PFF's first official sale, despite being the first club to use their numbers. After having his first bit of success talking with the Giants, Neil started calling other teams about player participation data, and in October 2010 the Chicago Bears paid PFF $1,400 for the data. Neil still has the check in his office.

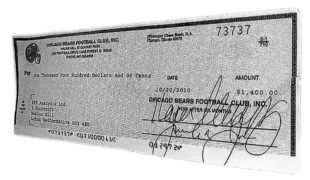

The Chicago Bears were the first team to pay for PFF's data. Neil Hornsby still has the check framed in his office.

It's not a sure thing that PFF's player participation would have caught on around the NFL without Nathan Jahnke, the king of player tracking. Imagine growing up never knowing that your secret talent was keeping count of everyone on a football field. That's Jahnke.

He built a decade-long career and was a vital part of the growth of Pro Football Focus by being the best at recording which guys were running around out on the field—a task that is much harder than it sounds.

When Jahnke came across PFF in 2010, he was a student at the University of Wisconsin–Eau Claire studying actuary science. The first question everyone asks when he talks about how he landed at PFF is *What the heck is actuary science?* In a sentence, it's using math to predict disasters. Or more politely phrased, "risk assessment." Insurance companies, for example, need to know the likelihood and frequency of bad things happening in order to set prices. State Farm does not decide that you have to pay $500 per month for car insurance based on a whim. It has actuaries calculate rates based on a bunch of different factors. Jahnke started out as a math major but decided being an actuary better suited him than teaching.

Sitting on Neil's patio furniture next to the pool, Jahnke fiddles with his oversized cargo shorts as he explains that actuaries generally make a bunch of money, so his family was pretty happy that he was headed into that field. If you're good at risk assessment, you can have a long career and great financial stability and buy a nice house in a nice neighborhood. It's ironically not very risky, as far as career paths go. By his senior year, Jahnke had a paid internship and was on his way to calculating the world's disasters.

In college, he had become enthralled with all the nerdy football stuff the internet was starting to produce. Pro Football Reference had a blog run by a writer named Chase Stuart that looked back at the history of football statistics, and Jahnke couldn't get enough. He wanted to do something like that, so he got started doing some charting work for one of the earliest football analytics websites, Football Outsiders.

"I quickly became aware that in order to do better than what any of these people are doing you need more data than what they have," Jahnke said.

He went on the hunt for play-by-play data, figuring that he could break some mathematical ground of his own if he had a record of every play. In a Google search, Jahnke turned up Pro Football Focus. For him, it was like opening the doors to a beautiful palace. Inside there was play-by-play, player participation, and where every player lined up.

This is what you have to understand about the original members of Pro Football Focus: to the vast majority of the human population, stumbling upon a bunch of spreadsheets that indicate how many snaps a wide receiver took for the Jacksonville Jaguars would not be a turning point in their life. In fact, it might be the most boring thing they have ever heard. But Neil's foundational group was built with people who are different. Like a chess prodigy who can spend 12 hours a day at the board, Jahnke never grew tired of the things he could do with PFF's data.

When PFF started putting things behind a paywall, an idea by early web editor Jonathan Comey that would eventually pay incredible dividends, Jahnke saw a note on the website that PFF was looking for help with grading and charting player participation and anyone who came aboard would be able to use the data for free. He wasn't a rich actuary yet, and he wanted to get in on that.

Jahnke emailed Neil and got back a game to test his ability to track which players were on the field. He nailed it on the first try. Usually the first run at tracking goes like that scene in *The Matrix* in which Neo attempts to jump between two buildings and falls. Not for Jahnke. He quickly became the most accurate player tracker of the group.

Where this becomes important is that the data had to be perfectly accurate to gain traction with more teams beyond the Giants. In order to take the step from hobby to company, PFF needed people like Jahnke who were dead-eye trackers.

They also needed people who were on the brink of lunacy with how many games they could cover. Jahnke, for whatever reason, loved the challenge of testing his speed and accuracy. On winter break from college, he blasted through games, spending morning, noon, and night watching play after play and simply writing down who was on the field.

"I got to a point where I was doing it so quickly that by the time it got to the commercial break, I was able to finish everything from the previous drive," Jahnke said with a big grin. "That led me to start tweeting snap counts during the middle of games, so I was the first person to tweet out that kind of information since I had it earlier than everyone else."

It doesn't sound like a difficult task on its face, but the next time you watch a football game, try to name every player on the field on offense and defense. The offensive linemen are always the same but almost everyone else can be subbed in or out at any time and many of them are similarly sized. Jahnke built a spreadsheet with every player's glove color, sleeve length, and shoe-and-sock color combinations to help him identify which players were in the game.

The guy who wanted to go into a field that would make him a lot of money ended up doing games during the first year for no money. He was happy with the pool of data that he got to swim in and enjoyed being part of Neil's online band of football nuts. When he finished college, PFF started paying him per game and Jahnke used money saved up from an actuary internship to live in a house with six friends in Eau Claire.

Nathan Jahnke's gift for tracking NFL player participation sparked a career in key roles at PFF.

His parents were skeptical when he didn't take a "real" job out of college.

"They were like, 'Maybe on the side you should still study for some actuary exams just in case this doesn't work out,'" Jahnke said. "And I was like, 'No, this is going to work out.'"

Neil says it wasn't that uncommon for family members of the Originals to think that some madman overseas had dragged their kids into a football cult and overtaken their lives. Try explaining to mom that you are bailing on the thing you just acquired a four-year degree to do so you can make spreadsheets of NFL players' accessories.

But it wasn't long before Jahnke turned out to be right and became the first full-time PFF employee on American soil. In subsequent years he turned into an integral part of the mathematical elements that would come along, like the development of the grading system, and he became Neil's trusted hiring manager. He was responsible for bringing dozens of people onboard as the company exploded between 2010 and '20, many of whom have taken PFF to new heights behind the scenes and in the front-facing media efforts that have earned them millions.

Jahnke helped create the larger-scale data collection process, including advanced player participation, which shows things like which gap a defensive linemen lined up over. He managed all the data collectors at one point, making sure games got done on time. Then he moved over to the analytics side of things, where he was key in changing over the grading system from plus-minus to a 1–100 scale. He switched over from there to being the senior software engineer, where he guided the IT people, who are less football inclined, to building models within PFF Ultimate. Recently, to tie it all back together to where it started with his football fandom, he became the senior fantasy analyst.

And it all started because he was good at spotting which dudes were on the field.

That's Nathan. In high school, he created a project to rank the best NFL players of all time. He watched old NFL Films videos from the 1960s and '70s to learn about the greatest players and then formed a system of comparing their arguments to be on his list using Pro Bowls, All-Pro nods, and wins—accolades he would never use now. Jerry Rice, Reggie White, and Joe Montana came out on the top of his list, he recalls. Nathan laughs about how PFF's yearly Top 100 lists became marathon phone conversations of a bunch of people trying to figure out which players were the best in the same way he did for his high school project.

When he thinks back on it, chasing a career in sports data should have been obvious, but nobody knew then that was even a viable option. Still, he might have gone in the actuary direction if not for his belief in Neil.

"He seemed really invested in wanting me to be involved with the company," Nathan said. "That meant a lot to me, and I think it drew in these people who were like-minded and willing to have really detailed conversations about football and every aspect of what we're doing as a company."

Chapter 4

REVENUE AND COMPETITION

B Y November 2009, the web clicks that were once only coming via Pro Football Focus' own writers were starting to accumulate from the rest of the world. Neil Hornsby could sense the momentum, and his business senses started tingling. He held a meeting to lay out goals, including getting 100 web visits per day and more than 10 media mentions before the NFL draft in April 2010. By the following summer, the site was gaining more than 700 visitors per day and receiving buzz from the mainstream media seemingly on a daily basis.

In a PowerPoint presentation, Neil wrote in the meeting notes, "[Football Outsiders] charges $75 for 1/10 of the information we produce...why should the NFL pay for our stuff when they can get it for nothing?" They decided to break up the subscriptions into different categories: just stats, stats and participation data, and fantasy premium.

He also wrote, "We make no money from what we do...untenable moving forward."

In late August, Neil sent out another update with praise for the PFF official Twitter account and talked about advertising and creating an iPhone app. Neil's other hope was to create a group of

32 "correspondents" who could cover each team for PFF through a data-driven lens. While that didn't come to fruition, and the app didn't launch until 2022, he would soon be able to get his people paid.

The first major influx of revenue for Pro Football Focus did not come from an NFL team. It came in 2011 from ESPN's Stats and Information department. In the early 2010s, ESPN was in the beginnings of an effort to go all-in on NFL coverage, especially online. It wasn't far away from creating NFL Nation, which was essentially the same idea that Neil had with a reporter in every city and aimed to bolster their package of statistics and data-driven analysis to reflect growth in those areas in other sports, like baseball and basketball.

Rather than mix and match numbers like passing yards and touchdowns, ESPN wanted to be able to give more detailed stats like how long it took for the quarterback to throw the ball after it had been snapped and have more articles from stats-savvy contributors breaking these things down. Neil's team had already been building more and more details about each into their tracking, going beyond player participation and grading. In the late August 2010 update, he asked for more specifics about each play. People who were grading games would note the routes run by receivers; who rushed the passer; whether passes were thrown deep, intermediate, or short; and numerous other elements that nobody had ever covered before.

ESPN had signed a contract with Football Outsiders in 2008 to use some of its metrics that were more formula-based, using box score numbers that could be more revealing than traditional stats. They wanted more.

ESPN offered Neil $70,000 over a year.

"It was like, 'whoa,'" Neil said. "Whoa!"

Neil's contracting job kept his expensive hobby afloat, but he was still paying for his ex-wife and children. The contract with ESPN would allow Neil to get the Originals paid and produce more data than he ever imagined.

"All I want to do is do more games, more grades, more data, because still the most exciting thing to me at that stage was pressing a button and a set of games combing through for a set of plays," Neil said. "This $70,000 allowed us to reinvest that money in people to get things done more quickly. None of that money is coming to me, but I didn't care. It just meant the company could last longer and we could do more things."

Football Outsiders felt Neil's pet project was encroaching on their turf, and Neil got his first taste of the competitive world of sports media.

Neil was told during a trip to ESPN that Football Outsiders founder Aaron Schatz had been trying to undermine their deal by telling them not to work with a "rich English dilettante." Those words remain in Neil's Twitter profile to this day.

PFF jabbed back, producing an ad that said, "No obscure formulas. When you watch 250 hours of tape each week, you don't have to guess."

Before he started Football Outsiders in July 2003, Schatz had a resume that read like a Mad Lib. He got a degree in economics from Brown University. He worked as music director at WKRO in Daytona Beach, Florida, and then got a job with the search engine Lycos.com. In 2002, Schatz was flustered by a local columnist asserting that the New England Patriots missed the postseason because they failed to establish the run, so he decided to look into it.

Schatz remembered the career of Bill James, often recognized as the founder of baseball's sabermetrics movement, had spawned from gathering and organizing box score statistics, so he decided to do the same. He created his own database and looked at whether teams that ran early in games had more success. His intuition that they did not turned out to be correct.

"When I was done with this, I had a database of every play from the 2002 NFL season and I'm like, 'What else can I do with this?'" Schatz said over the phone.

What he did was begin to recreate the statistics from the groundbreaking book *Hidden Game of Football*, which was written by three statisticians in 1988 and included advanced numbers never seen before in football, including "success rate," which Schatz eventually developed into his DVOA stat that is still often cited by football reporters and analysts.

When sports sites that he knew through his job at Lycos didn't bite on running his new numbers, Schatz got together with some of his fraternity brothers from Brown who knew how to program websites and launched Football Outsiders on July 30, 2003.

There was nothing like it back then. There were some sites that were tangentially similar, but not exactly. Some focused on gambling, some on fantasy football—but nothing that was entirely focused on football analytics for fans who wanted to understand the game in a different way from whatever the TV color commentator or local columnist was writing.

When the dot-com bubble burst, Schatz lost his job at Lycos. He got an offer to work at Google but didn't want to move to Mountain View, California, so he decided to give Football Outsiders a go as a career. That was in February 2004. By September of the same year, he made it a full-time job by combining Football Outsiders with gigs at ESPN Page 2 and an alternative newspaper called the *New York Sun*, which decided its best chance to compete with the other New York papers was to have stats-based writing rather than trying to employ beat reporters for every team.

Michael Lewis' *Moneyball* being published in 2003 helped give Football Outsiders a boost. Football fans looked for their version of Bill James and Baseball Prospectus and found it in Schatz and his crew of writers, which steadily grew into an all-star team. Current ProFootballTalk writer Michael David Smith came aboard first. ESPN's Bill Barnwell was in Schatz's fantasy baseball league. Mike Tanier and Doug Farrar found the site and offered to get involved. They have each gone on to have accomplished football writing careers.

"I have quite the coaching tree," Schatz said. "I think I've been good at helping people hone their craft. We have a lot of big people who have come out of Football Outsiders."

In 2005, Schatz wanted to chart games and provide statistics that had never been seen before in the NFL, such as which cornerbacks gave up the most yards per pass attempt into their coverage. But it took forever to get all the games tracked and produce the data. Another analytics pioneer, KC Joyner, also had plans to chart games and sell the numbers to teams. But executing the idea was a different story.

"All I had was a bunch of volunteers…and I had no seed capital money to pay them," Schatz said.

Schatz feels that Neil gained his edge through having more resources to pay people to chart games, which resulted in PFF charting games quicker, gaining the attention of teams, and getting more money to pay more trackers. And off they went. That sentiment has shades of truth because Neil did pay some people like Ben Stockwell and Sam Monson, but most people started on a volunteer basis. That was more a testament to Hornsby's organizational skills and the sheer luck of landing uniquely obsessive people like himself.

"He wasn't Elon Musk where he could do whatever, but it is an inside joke of the company because none of us were making any money," PFF's Mike Parker said. "We were all basically doing this poor."

Schatz also didn't believe in the grading system. He acknowledges now that it has been proven to be predictive of future performance, but at its launch he didn't trust the concept that random football fans could watch the games and understand enough to score the players accurately.

"The idea that he had that no one else had was the grading and that was very popular with a lot of people in the media because even if you questioned how accurate the grades were, if you wanted to write about a guard, there were no stats," Schatz said. "All you had was PFF grades, so of course you quoted them because you had nothing else. What else were you going to use? That is an idea that I never had. That's a unique idea that Neil had. The idea of charting games and selling data to teams, I had that idea too."

Schatz and Hornsby talked a few times. Hornsby described their conversations as Schatz saying he didn't like what PFF was doing but wanted to use some of their data.

Schatz sees now that it would have been beneficial to join forces with PFF. That's because Football Outsiders has long been left behind by PFF in terms of company size.

"They are much larger than us," Schatz said. "I'm sure there was a time when Coca-Cola and RC Cola were the same size. And there are still some people who really, really like RC Cola."

There is a significant fundamental difference between Schatz and Hornsby: One of them wanted to change the way people talked about the NFL in the media; the other wanted more football data. Schatz wanted to be football's Bill James. Neil didn't give a shit about influencing the way fans looked at the game. After landing the ESPN contract, Neil's goal was to figure out more ways to sell his data.

"I think [Aaron Schatz's] main problem was that he made it too much about him and not enough about the other people and therefore lost a ton of good people," Neil said. "If you look at a lot of the Football Outsiders people and where they went, there's a really good track record of people going through there, but Aaron needed to find a way to keep them. I think this was always 'Aaron Schatz's Football Outsiders' to him, and the first part of that was more important than the Football Outsiders piece."

Schatz maintains that if he had the money to invest in game trackers and pay his writers more, things would have gone differently. Neil would argue that ideas are nothing without execution.

PFF's success isn't easy for Schatz to reckon with. In some ways he sees himself as the other guy who was discovering the lightbulb at the same time as Thomas Edison. In reality, he's more like the scientists who discovered electric light was possible 40 years before Edison did.

"I think you have Football Outsiders setting the table—they were building this up like, 'Hey, people, this is happening.'" Parker said. "So they deserve a lot of credit for being a pioneer in the space with the idea of analyzing data like Bill James and *Moneyball*."

Being a football analytics pioneer doesn't pay as well as building a data company that works with all 32 teams. But Schatz's work has echoes everywhere. Every time a head coach calls for his team to "establish the run," reporters roll their eyes, rather than nodding in agreement. If you aren't using data to back arguments when writing or talking about football, you're a dinosaur. Football Outsiders started that ball rolling when Schatz and his crew began publishing data-driven articles.

"I started Football Outsiders to change the way that the game was covered," Schatz. "I am an entertainer at heart. I was a radio personality. I'm a writer. If any of my work changed how teams actually ran themselves that was awesome but my big thing was changing the media…. You have beat writers quoting us, quoting PFF, you have them charting games themselves for the game they cover, you have someone like Mina Kimes on NFL Live, you have people like Kevin Seifert and Mike Sando who are national reporters using analytics in their articles… the writers are really advanced compared to where they used to be."

Schatz is now open to working with PFF, appearing on their podcasts and vice versa. He stated appreciation for the studies they have published recently looking deep into analytics of the game and even gave credence to the parts of the grading system that have proven predictive over time. He tries to separate thinking about how things could have been different from what he thinks of PFF now.

"I have a lot of respect for what they've built," Schatz said.

Neil Hornsby and Aaron Schatz were hardly the only ones who had the idea to create football data companies in the 2000s.

EdjSports was co-founded by Frank Frigo, who was a backgammon world champion and worked in commodity markets structuring wholesale energy transactions. Frigo built his first football simulation model, called "Zeus," in 2001, right around the time Billy Beane was winning with the Moneyball Oakland A's. EdjSports was launched in 2013 with its specialty being in-game decision-making. Edj's model uses historical play-by-play data and Football Outsiders' DVOA to assess a team's chance of winning at any given moment and how it changes with each decision the coach makes (e.g., going for it on fourth down, kicking a field goal, calling timeout).

"Every individual decision can be measured in that context and if you don't obsess about scoring on a possession or the final score, you get some amazing insights about how to improve your win probability," Frigo told me in 2021 for a Purple Insider article about in-game decisions. "There are often situations in a game that are very high leverage that the model will say, 'Do this because it improves your win probability.'

The Eagles used EdjSports' data in part to influence their decisions to go for fourth downs during their run to the 2017 Super Bowl. In 2018, EdjSports acquired Football Outsiders.

EdjSports wasn't trying to accomplish the same things that PFF was when it was searching for relevancy in the NFL but they were/are part of the vast competition for teams' attention when it comes to selling data and analysis. The same goes for STATS Inc.

In the early 1980s, John Dewan, an actuary who studied mathematics and computer science at Loyola University, helped Bill James launch Project Scoresheet by building data-collecting software for the baseball analytics legend. Soon after that he co-founded STATS Inc., which grew over the years in the baseball space by gathering box scores and presenting them in ways that made it possible to study the game differently than traditional pitching win-loss record and hitter batting average. One example was creating zones on the field to study fielders' ability to save runs. In 2000, Fox Sports bought STATS Inc. and it expanded to sports outside of baseball. In 2011 STATS Inc. formed an agreement with the video company XOS to include football data when selling to teams.

That set the stage for PFF gaining more traction with teams.

"When we started having conversations with the teams around 2013–2014, it was year three or year four of STATS Inc. trying to sell these teams like, 'you need data, you need data,' and all we had to do was convince teams that our data was better than theirs," Parker said.

STATS Inc. (now known as STATS Perform after merging with Perform Content) still has football products. It touts a relationship with the New England Patriots on its website and specifically advertises offensive line metrics and yardage over expected stats.

Overall, STATS is a much bigger company than PFF, working with soccer and rugby clubs and NBA, MLB, and NHL teams. It has significant media deals with ESPN, Google, and Bet365 and has contracts with sportsbooks, but it was not able to hold off PFF from taking over as the league's data provider.

"We were more expensive because our overhead was higher and we had to charge more," Parker said. "We had to take down the incumbent by also being more expensive, which as you can imagine is extra hard."

Parker says that the reason they were able to gain an edge with football teams in the competitive data world was by communicating with teams and understanding their specific needs.

"STATS Inc. was basically saying, we'll give you this data and you figure it out. They didn't want the relationships; as long as checks were clearing, they didn't want anyone to call," he said.

The human touch has always been their advantage. Who else could put together the team of individuals charting games? The NFL recently took another avenue, which concerned PFF: digital tracking data called "Next Gen Stats." It became a common theme that PFF would hear, "You guys are done once tracking data comes along,"

Instead, teams were overwhelmed by the pile of data dumped on them from digital trackers placed in players' pads, and it became part of PFF's value to clubs to work with the new numbers.

"We had built analysis tools that Next Gen Stats had not built and were better than what they were building," data scientist Eric Eager said. "The people with the teams, they don't have the time to do the research that we do. They are doing a lot of grindy work.... I think that's what makes this company enduring despite having lots of competition—we can go into a room with a team and say, 'Let us take this off your plate.'"

Companies like STATS Inc. and EdjSports are just the tip of the iceberg when it comes to competition for PFF. So long as NFL and college football teams are desperate for an advantage, they will always be willing to listen. You can bet there is another Neil Hornsby somewhere right now looking for a way to provide a better product to NFL teams and a better analytics-based website for fans to consume.

Chapter 5

GOING ALL-IN ON PFF

I N EARLY 2012, PFF's momentum was about to get kicked into high gear with an article in the *Wall Street Journal* titled, "In Super Bowl, Giants Go Long for a Number Cruncher."

Writer Reed Albergotti was enthused about the piece because he'd landed the "A-head" story on the front page for that day's paper.

"Every day there is a quirky story on the front page," Albergotti said over the phone. "Your favorite thing to do if you're a *Wall Street Journal* reporter is write the A-head for the day because you get on Page 1, but it's not news, it's this quirky fun story on the front page. I pitched it as, 'You've never heard of this British guy who knows more about football than anyone in the U.S.'"

The story introduced Neil Hornsby to the world. The lede called Neil the Giants' "secret strategist."

Albergotti discovered Neil through Peter King. He was blown away by the idea that King, one of the football universe's most accomplished writers, was getting ideas and information from a random British guy who wasn't involved in football as a player, coach, or executive. Albergotti wanted in with King's secret Brit.

Albergotti was writing a football column with the goal of bringing more insight than your average narrative-based football columnist or reporter. The *Wall Street Journal* wanted an analytical approach to sports, so Albergotti had the idea to set up DirectTV at his desk and watch every game. For an entire year, he picked out one play that caught his eye and wrote about it. He would get a hold of the player or coach involved and have them break down what happened.

"If you actually watch football and what's happening with the offensive line and all the stuff that's away from the ball is super important and interesting," Albergotti said. "So I called Neil and he's like, 'We just watch every single player on every single play and we chart it and we have all these statistics.'"

Albergotti was taken aback. How was that possible?

"At the time everyone would say, 'You could never do Moneyball with football because there aren't enough games, there aren't enough statistics, there aren't enough plays,' and that was the conventional wisdom," Albergotti said.

Albergotti's career has taken him a lot of different places, including writing the groundbreaking book on Lance Armstrong *Wheelmen*, but he's a football guy at heart. His grandparents were Minnesota Vikings season ticket holders from day one, literally, of the franchise in 1960. They were known for two things: running a bridal store in downtown Minneapolis called Rush's Bridal and loving the Vikings. His grandfather would sneak liquor into the games in a flask that he'd created by hollowing out binoculars and his grandmother, the biggest Viking nut in the family, would wear a Vikings helmet with massive golden braids attached. When he was growing up Albergotti played offensive line, so he was intrigued by the idea that Pro Football Focus could evaluate the guys in the trenches. He thought all the time about the positions that went largely unnoticed by TV viewers who were watching the ball.

Talking with Neil first prompted Albergotti to write an article about how the NFL did not want fans to see the same "All-22" film that the coaches were privy to because the coaches couldn't stand the idea of fans and media seeing enough to intelligently critique their decisions.

"The NFL was really pissed about that article," Albergotti said, laughing.

But that article led to the NFL releasing the All-22 film to the public.

Albergotti started calling Neil often. He would ask Neil what he was seeing as far as trends in the data. Neil sent Albergotti offensive line spreadsheets that he would have open when watching games. He couldn't get enough of Neil's numbers, in part because the state of football data was so unfulfilling.

"I thought he was on to something," Albergotti said. "If you write about football and you're trying to write in an analytical way, you're always looking for data, and data is the chocolate sprinkles for your articles. Data always sounds so good. It makes it sound so well researched and you can back up your idea, but half the time the data in football was a little bit shaky. You would base these articles on it, but sometimes the data wasn't really that great. But it was data, so you used it. But his data, no one was doing anything like that."

After writing a number of articles inspired by Neil and his data, Albergotti decided it was time to give credit where credit was due.

"I was like, I have to write a story about this guy.... This guy is fascinating. He's this British guy, you'd never think he would think of this idea," Albergotti said. "I wanted people to know who he was."

The article officially put PFF on the map. The Jacksonville Jaguars, Carolina Panthers, and Miami Dolphins called Neil after reading the article and it led to several new contracts. More than anything, it established credibility. The Giants pulled off an upset winning the Super Bowl and PFF had been involved. For the first time, Neil felt like his little garage band was turning into something that could be big.

Albergotti saw it as the turning of a corner in football, even if many inside the game weren't ready for it.

"They had the Wizard Behind the Curtain attitude about football," Albergotti said. "People didn't want you to know how the game worked. I would ask players about play-calling and they didn't want to talk about it, and the data you did find was very outsider-y, not data that people inside of the game would really use."

"The NFL was growing and they had this great thing, and they didn't want to mess with it. This kind of revolution you're talking about was not very welcome and I encountered that defensiveness all the time. People didn't want you asking those types of questions at all. It was almost like the NFL had this aversion to an intellectual take on the game."

Albergotti eventually moved to the white-collar crime beat and reached out to Neil from time to time. When I talked to

THE WALL STREET JOURNAL.

Home   World   U.S.   Politics   Economy   Business   Tech   Markets   Opinion   Books & Arts   Real Estate   Life

In Super Bowl, Giants Go Long for a Number Cruncher
Football Novice From England Studies Footage, Supplies Data

By Reed Albergotti
February 4, 2012

🖨 PRINT   aA TEXT

INDIANAPOLIS—A secret strategist for the New York Giants won't be in Indianapolis for Sunday's Super Bowl bout against the New England Patriots. He won't even be in the U.S.

Neil Hornsby will be watching the game on television from his home about 30 miles from London. A north England native, Mr. Hornsby never played a down of football. Not until the age of 42 did he attend his first professional football game. Yet from watching games broadcast over the Internet, he has compiled research and analysis that the Giants and several other teams used this season to prepare for their opponents.

Reed Albergotti's *Wall Street Journal* article introduced Neil Hornsby and PFF to the masses—and earned them new business from teams.

Albergotti, he had no idea what PFF had become, but he wasn't surprised to find out.

"I thought that's what readers wanted," Albergotti said. "Tell me something I didn't know about this game."

The excitement of the article, the Giants' Super Bowl win, and the growth of the company were conflicting for Neil. The WSJ article increased Neil's gnawing feeling that this could be his career, and he badly wanted to find out if he was right.

If there was any time to go all-in on PFF, it was now. The PFF team was getting stronger and people on the outside were starting to see what they were doing. Financially, the mortgage was finally paid off and Neil's family life was stable.

In early 2012, Neil decided to have a conversation with Claire that turned out to be a crossroads moment in his life.

"Darling, I'd like to give this football thing a go full time," he told Claire.

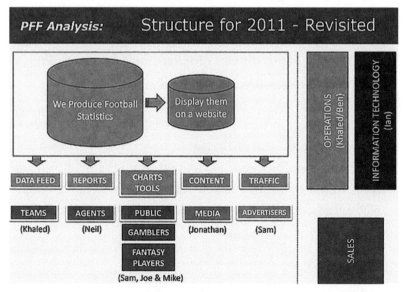

A slide showing the company structure from one of Neil Hornsby's meetings with the early PFF crew.

Neil laid out for his wife what that would mean for them.

"With a fair wind and everything going to plan we can maybe make this into a business where I can maybe earn $30,000 or $40,000 a year and just enjoy the rest of my life as opposed to doing it in a job that I don't like," he explained to Claire, sitting on their back patio.

In a way, he felt weird asking if she would be onboard. She had continued working after they had both boys, which essentially helped pay for Neil's first marriage. Now, at the very moment he was getting ahead, he was proposing that his pay be cut by 90 percent and she would continue to carry a financial burden.

"You weren't exactly selling it," she said, laughing softly, as the three of us chatted for this book in 2021.

Claire told him that if he wanted to chase this dream job, he should give it a shot.

"I just said that he needed to do what he needed to do," Claire said. "Was it disappointing that I couldn't give up work when I was getting to that point where I would have liked to and maybe spend more time with the kids? But I just knew that if he didn't do it, he'd regret it. That wasn't going to be good. I didn't even have to think about it. It was, 'Yeah, let's do it.'"

She remembered talking to Reed Albergotti for his story and being asked what she thought of his business idea.

"I said, genuinely, I don't know football so I can't really have a view on it as a business because we never really sat down and talked about it as a business," Claire said. "I said, 'I trust Neil and that's all I need to know.' I remember having that conversation."

Neil admits that if she had vetoed the idea to put his full-time efforts into PFF he would have let it go.

"If she would have said, 'You can't do this,' I would have said OK," Neil said. "I would have resented it every single second and it might have led to a lot of problems, but I would have always gone with what she said."

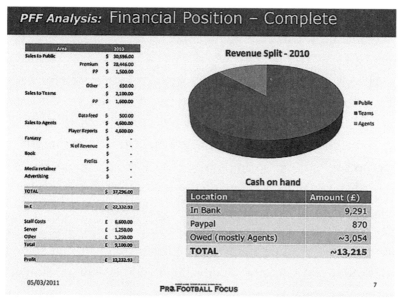

Another slide from a company meeting showing PFF's revenue sources.

For Neil, it wasn't just an opportunity to play in a football sandbox as his full-time job. It was deeper than that. It was a chance to escape the rat race and do something that would carry a greater meaning to him and the Originals. This was about what would make him happy for the remainder of his working life.

"If you could do something that you were the happiest in the world at and it was going to earn you just enough to survive, why the hell wouldn't you do it?" Neil said. "You could be a person like I was who was potentially getting paid a lot more money than they needed but wasn't happy. Which is a better scenario?"

Claire giving the green light for Neil to focus solely on PFF also triggered another key part of PFF's rapid growth: Neil turned from a football fan into a football businessman. His entire career had been leading teams of workers, organizing, and executing. Between the time he first decided to grade a game and 2012, he'd been doing all of that with PFF but only in the same way someone is president of their rotary club. Now he was set to transition from part-time boss, part-time football fan to the head of a start-up company.

He felt strongly that the circumstances were set up for success from the perspective of structuring PFF. Not just because the company was gaining notoriety but because people working on something they love is simply different from working for a paycheck.

"When you're working in a [corporation], you feel like a person who is trying to implement rules that you don't believe in," Neil said. "Even as a senior manager within a [corporation], you are still implementing rules that are brought down from somebody's idea of what shareholder value is and inevitably it's linked to bonuses which are linked to the short term which are linked to people doing well in the short term."

"Corporations generally, unless they're really smart, unless they're one of the great enduring companies, are constantly robbing from Peter to pay Paul because they're constantly trying to bring forward results to make themselves look good now rather than worrying about what happens in the future," Neil continued.

He didn't want to be that way. He wanted something that would last rather than a company that was constantly rotating people in and out based on last month's revenue.

"If somebody said to me, 'You can only give me one thing, what would be at the root of PFF's success so far?' My answer would be, 'It's because we tried to do great things, we didn't try to make money.'"

While Neil didn't set out to make money, when he made PFF his full-time job, he knew he needed to make more money. Sometimes you need a little luck to get from Point A to Point B, and for Neil that came in the form of an offer from Peter King to go on a training camp tour.

PFF Analysis: What could we have done better?

○ We are not running PFF as a Company financially
  - *Too much talk of money – "What's in it for me?" – People should know*
  - *Inherent unfairness in hours worked to returns. Effort/success should = Reward*
  - *Dishing out shares year on year is not sustainable*

○ Error Trapping
  - *Large amounts of errors getting through*
  - *Possible credibility gap*
  - *Large amounts of rework required*
  - *Taking time away from revenue generation*

○ Strategy
  - *What were we REALLY trying to achieve?*
  - *Did we focus our efforts correctly?*
  - *Did we make best use of our resources?*

While PFF was just beginning, Neil Hornsby prioritized a high standard from his team of football fanatics.

In the late '90s/early 2000s, Peter's brother Ken lived in England and worked for a hospitality company called Whitbread. Coincidentally, Neil was working for Whitbread at the time, and they met during a company social event.

"I heard the American accent, and I didn't get many Americans to talk to back in the day," Neil said. "I said, do you like football at all?"

At one point it came up that Ken was Peter's brother. Imagine Neil's surprise that he'd run into the brother of a famous NFL writer. Imagine Ken's surprise that he found someone in England who knew American football well enough to know the name Peter King. Most didn't know the name Dan Marino, much less that of a sportswriter.

"We'd probably [met] two or three times before [Ken] said, 'Do you know my brother at all?'" Hornsby said. "I said, 'Who's your brother?' He said, 'Peter King.' I said, 'You're joking.' He said, 'Peter King is my brother.' Of course I know who he is; he's one of my favorite sportswriters. He and Dr. Z are my favorite sportswriters in football."

Ken and Neil spent time together, going to cricket matches and talking football. They eventually started a contest picking NFL games. The loser had to buy tickets to the next cricket match.

Neil got to know Ken well enough to ask him a favor: Could he talk to Peter King? Peter had included an offensive lineman named Jeremy Trueblood in his All-Pro team, and Neil was beside himself. The PFF grading system may have still been in its early stages, but the grades were showing Trueblood as one of the worst linemen in the NFL.

"My brother Ken said to me, 'There's this guy who is absolutely crazy about the NFL and talks about it all the time who analyzes the games, and on your midseason All-Pro team you had a guy by the name of Jeremy Trueblood, a Tampa Bay offensive tackle, and Neil said it was a horrible pick and he wants to talk to you about it,'" King said over the phone.

"I figured that it's my brother, so I said OK. I got in touch with Neil; he was very polite, very nice, and he said, 'You're crazy, he's the worst tackle in the league, he's awful.' King said, 'How could you put him there?' I said, 'Well, I poll personnel guys and that's where I get most of my stuff.' And he goes, 'They're wrong; this guy is awful.'"

Peter and Neil stayed in touch and Peter kept his eye on PFF. Right around the time Neil was considering making PFF his full-time gig, Peter was getting set to go on his annual training camp tour.

"I was talking to Peter and he said he was going on a training camp tour. I went, 'You lucky bastard…I can't imagine having a job like yours where you just go around to training camps,'" Hornsby said. "[Peter] said it's a little bit harder than what you think."

Peter told Neil that if he met him in the Detroit airport at 6 AM the following Monday, Neil could come on his annual training camp tour and Peter would introduce him to people around the NFL.

Neil scrambled to finish up a consulting job and showed up in Detroit. He rode along for the NFC North visits. One of the memorable stops was Minnesota, where linebacker Chad Greenway was excited to learn that Neil's grading system found him to be underrated. Peter remembers Vikings general manager Rick Spielman being particularly wary about an outsider's ability to evaluate his players, but he was hardly alone.

"Everybody was dubious," King said. "In Minnesota there were a lot of people who said, 'You can't do that, you don't know what the assignment is for every player, how could you tell whether he did a good job or bad job.' There was immense skepticism of Neil on that trip."

At first, Neil took the criticism without much pushback.

"When you start a process and you're grading players and some general manager who has been doing this forever tells you that you can't do that, you have to take that seriously," Hornsby said.

But as he heard the same things from teams over and over, Neil started to feel that the critiques were for his benefit, rather than trying to tear him down.

"I got much better at asking questions," Hornsby said. "The last thing you want to come across as is defensive. If you come across as defensive, that guy goes, 'Fuck you, I'm not going to give you any more feedback,' and you're screwed."

Neil recalled one particular executive, Rob Rogers, who was with the Carolina Panthers at the time and now works as senior VP of football administration for the Washington Commanders, giving him feedback about offensive linemen. PFF had favored one of Carolina's guards over another, but Rogers pointed out to Neil that one of the guards was asked to make much more difficult blocks, which sometimes resulted in errors. To NFL evaluators, degree of difficulty was important.

Neil knew Rogers was right.

"We have to do something about it," he said. "We have to get more information. That's how we got better."

While Neil was networking, selling PFF's data and learning how to create a better product, Peter King was simply enjoying the company, having endless conversations with Neil during the long hours on the road.

"He thinks about the game in a way that is really interesting, he's open minded about what works and what doesn't work, and he's become a friend over the years," King said. "I admire the fact that he decided he wanted to do something, and he moved heaven and earth to try to do it and he's done it."

Neil, however, did not always enjoy Peter's driving.

"We're driving up through Green Bay through the middle of the night because he won't leave somewhere until he's got everything

One of the NFL's most accomplished writers, Peter King gave Pro Football Focus a shot in the arm before it was well known in the league.

he needs to get done and I remember we nearly died on the road because some deer ran out and he was tired, so he wasn't paying as much attention as he should be, and I'm shitting myself," Hornsby said, howling. "The one bad thing I'll say about Peter is that he's not the world's best driver."

Peter and Neil's summer adventures didn't end there. They went on future trips, including one memorable one to Arizona. They were driving from Flagstaff to Yuma and Peter needed to write, so he let Neil drive. The problem was that Neil wasn't insured to drive the car. Peter demanded that Neil keep the car under the speed limit while he penned his column to avoid any potential issues with the law.

"We're driving and he keeps on saying, 'Neil, you need to slow down.' I'm like five miles an hour over the speed limit," Hornsby said. "He keeps giving me this warning. We eventually get past Phoenix, and this is about the third warning. '*Pull over, Neil. Pull over.*' We know each other a bit by then, but he's still Peter King. He goes, 'I'm telling you for the last time, you cannot do this.' He's scolding a guy in his mid-forties about being over the speed limit."

Every time they get together, Neil recounts that story with Peter and they laugh harder than the last time he told it.

"I was always grateful," Hornsby said. "I have some wonderful stories. If Peter ever writes his story—and he should—I have a lot of very funny tales."

Well after the sun had gone down in Cincinnati, Neil was up past his bedtime looking through old files and reminiscing. He sent Peter a text: "Always grateful for what you have done to help us."

"He's a big part of PFF's story," Neil said.

Chapter 6

SAM AND STEVE
INTRODUCE PFF
TO THE WORLD

Bᴇ 2013, Pʀᴏ Fᴏᴏᴛʙᴀʟʟ Fᴏᴄᴜs had contracts with nearly one-third of the NFL, and the media world was starting to buy in to their expertise. If you google headlines involving PFF from that year, you'll find ESPN, the *Chicago Sun-Times*, Bleacher Report, Yahoo! Sports, and dozens of blogs that were exploding on the scene.

With their data in hand, Neil and the Originals were starting to make some discoveries. Unlike *Heinrich's Pro Preview* magazine, which was reporting off guesswork or what broadcasters said about players, PFF's data was revealing things about football that were groundbreaking for the time, and they were getting enough web traffic for fans and media to take notice. One of the early staples of the site was the Secret Superstars series, in which PFF spotlighted players who went under the traditional media radar but had analytical reasons to think they were better than their reputation. For example, Ben Stockwell wrote this about Buffalo Bills guard Andy Levitre in May 2012:

> Levitre's ability in pass protection at both guard and tackle
> cannot be questioned. Over the last two seasons whether

you look at our grades (+15.1) or the stats (35 total pressures allowed), he is amongst the elite pass protectors at
guard. Combined with clear improvements in his in-line
run blocking, and his consistent quality blocking in space,
Levitre is ready to use the 2012 season to break into the
NFL's upper echelon of guards.

A paragraph like this wouldn't look unusual to anyone in the
year 2022, but in 2012, it was mind-blowing to see quantitative
analysis of offensive linemen.

PFF's writers/graders Stockwell, Gordon McGuiness, Steve
Palazzolo, and Sam Monson started making statements that didn't
always sit well with football outlets. Players who were widely
praised were sometimes revealed to be overrated when studied
under the PFF microscope. Traditional ideas about the game, like
the value of running backs or run-stuffing middle linebackers, were
challenged. Traditional statistics like tackles or passer rating came
under scrutiny from PFF when they didn't always tell the story.

It wasn't until a few years later that PFF's data would get under
the skin of the mainstream and push the company's media side
into the stratosphere, but in its relative infancy PFF's revelations
caught the eye of writer Kevin Clark.

Since starting at the *Wall Street Journal* in 2010, Clark has
become one of the media's top thought leaders on football
analytics. He has written dozens upon dozens of data-influenced
articles that shaped the way fans see the game. In 2022, he hosted
a panel on football analytics at the MIT Sloan Sports Analytics
Conference.

When Clark was hired by the *Wall Street Journal*, his first job
was to write about the New York Knicks. He quickly figured out
that he was the smallest fish in the Big Apple basketball pond with
longtime writers like Frank Isola, Marc Berman, and Alan Hahn

dominating the Knicks beat. Those guys could get 15 NBA head coaches on the phone in an hour if they wanted to write a story. Clark didn't know anybody to call. So he started to talk to other people around the team, namely people on the Knicks analytics staff. Basketball wasn't quite ready to explode into the data-driven game we know now with Steph Curry bombing three-pointers from all areas of the court, but it was still far ahead of football in the early 2010s. You could find things like how a player performed on the pick and roll, which felt revolutionary.

The Knicks had acquired Carmelo Anthony and Amar'e Stoudemire the previous year and fans were expecting the two stars to take the Knicks back to the glory years of Patrick Ewing and John Starks. But the analytics folks were skeptical.

"People were so swept up by the star power with Amar'e and Carmelo being superstars that they thought they were going to take on the Miami Heat, and that just wasn't the case, it wasn't even close to the case, and the only reason I was confident in talking about that was because the data guys were 100 percent sure about that," Clark said on a Zoom call from his New York apartment. "I thought that was really fascinating."

In 2010–11 and 2011–12, the Knicks made the playoffs but were knocked out in the first round each time. Clark was captivated by the way in which the numbers told him what was going to happen before it happened. What's better for a reporter than being given a crystal ball? He found other uses to deploy the data in ways few reporters ever have: by combining them with interviews inside the locker room. He asked Carmelo why the statistics said he was so good at spot-up jumpers, and it turned into a memorable story. Clark was hooked.

In 2012, he moved from the Knicks beat to cover the NFL. Enter PFF.

"I remember there were so many things that I thought about football that PFF quickly taught me were wrong," Clark said.

The first time he talked with Neil Hornsby was for a story about tackle statistics. Before the PFF era, linebackers were judged by how many tackles they amassed in a year. Tackle leaders got Pro Bowl nods and adulation from broadcasts. But PFF found that tackle statistics were a very bad way of evaluating a linebacker because they provided no context. Did the guy tackle someone in the backfield or 20 yards down the field? Also, as Clark found out from Neil, NFL stat keepers were super bad at figuring out which player actually made the play.

"It was so funny to me because I grew up in an era, I was young in the '90s, but I remember that era was like, 'Oh my god, Brian Urlacher has 105 tackles, what a machine,'" Clark said. "And then this company called PFF that's telling you so many of the counting stats are either wrong or they didn't matter. I got to know them through that and that helped me."

Because Clark was one of the few football writers applying numbers beyond the surface level, people around the league wanted to talk with him about it. While organizations and the league at large hadn't yet gone all-in on spreadsheets and algorithms, there were early adopters in the NFL who were just as captivated as Clark.

"I was learning deep, deep, deep football in 2012, 2013, 2014, and I couldn't imagine a better time to do it up to that point because I had PFF back-check any of the old theories," he said. "I remember a position coach told me that the best thing about analytics was that it gave you a way to test old theories that you'd always had."

Clark wanted to test all the theories and find some new ones as well. He noticed that many reporters were starting to cite PFF grades but few were asking the people playing the game about the things that the data revealed. Clark saw data from PFF showing that certain teams were highly successful in the first two seconds of a play, so he went in search of answers for why that might be. He found all sorts of new avenues to tell the story of the NFL through data.

"Letting data take you places that you didn't expect to go is not a bad storytelling path," he said.

Every year Clark would do a training camp tour in which he wrote features about the clubs that he visited. As he leaned more into writing about numbers, he would often ask decision-makers how they were applying analytics.

"I'd talk to half the teams about analytics and back then in 2013, 2014, 2015, you either got eyerolls or blank stares from the vast majority of teams," Clark said. "There were four or five teams that were always doing it. I always joke that New England—if New England was upfront like the Oakland A's were about how much they use analytics, analytics would have been in football 20 years ago. They are so secretive that nobody knew what they were doing, and they still don't know what they're doing. That part hurt the analytics movement a little bit. The team that was awesome at using them kept it an absolute secret. There was no Moneyball football because NFL GMs don't ever want to say what their edge is. But I will say that back then most teams were not taking it seriously."

Clark sees the Eagles' 2017 Super Bowl victory—the one where the game-winning play was drawn up using PFF Ultimate—as a turning point toward many teams realizing they needed to adapt or die.

"Coaches and GMs and front-office people hid behind the idea that there had always been analytics in football, and that was true, the big line was, 'The Combine is analytics, the 40 is analytics, the explosion scores that front offices have between the vertical jump, the broad jump, that's analytics, we've been doing analytics for years,'" Clark explained. "It took a number of years for teams to understand that analytics could help them beyond that. I think there was a lot of hesitancy. A lot of people were scared that the rules of engagement were changing and that if they weren't going to be the top GM or whatever if they had to go through all this data and I think they didn't even give it a shot."

In 2019, Clark opened his email one day to find a note from an NFL general manager whom he barely knew. Unprompted, the GM outlined how his team was using analytics. The GM just wanted Clark to know that they were up to date.

"You saw that switch," he said. "Even if I don't get analytics, I'm going to say I get analytics."

"There were so many things that were changing about the sport in that era and PFF was a huge part of that," Clark continued. "It was reverberating through the front offices and coaching staffs in a way that was really fascinating because I don't think a lot of people were ready for it at that point."

The outside world was starting to get it as well.

With the NFL starting to come around on using data to drive its decisions, there was more interest in finding out where these numbers were coming from and what they meant for the futures of their teams.

It wasn't Neil Hornsby who played the role of ambassador to NFL fans for the analytics cause for PFF in the early 2010s. Instead, Sam Monson and Steve Palazzolo became the faces of all things PFF to the outside world.

Monson was one of the Originals who came from the message board era of the internet. It would be hard to explain to someone who was born after the year 1998 that there was a universe before Facebook, Twitter, Instagram, and TikTok where all these things happened in giant forums that moved at a slower pace and you didn't get a choice about whose opinions you were reading.

"Neil had this idea and had this system that he wanted to introduce and needed manpower and needed people to do games; otherwise, the whole thing is a waste of time," Monson said. "When the NFL is still a niche sport in the UK, there aren't a ton of those people growing on trees, especially not in your everyday social circles. Where am I going to find people that know football that I can trust? And the answer was the message boards."

Monson had just finished college and was "bumbling around" trying to figure out what in god's name he was going to do with a history and politics degree. He was happy to have improved his critical thinking abilities but unhappy to find out that his education didn't qualify him for any particular career path. Monson started down the path to becoming a barrister, which is like a trial attorney in the U.S., but discovered that you don't get to be like Jack Nicholson in *A Few Good Men*. It's more research and paperwork than yelling, "Do you want the truth? You can't handle the truth!"

When Neil asked him if he'd like to get involved with his data project, Monson decided to jump in. He started with player participation, like everybody else. He was coaching kids' rugby, working on a journalism master's degree, and feeling waves of resentment toward people who knew what they wanted to be from an early age. He explained that despite being from Ireland, he did a lot of his formative education in England, where students cut down their course schedule to focus on particular areas that would prepare them for college. Monson's father was a surgeon, so he considered medicine, but history was his best subject, so he went in that direction. Really his feeling was, "How the hell should I know what I want to be now?"

Monson understood that his love for the NFL was unusual. Because of his father's profession, his family spent time in different places growing up, including Minnesota when he was seven years old. The Vikings had just made their infamous Herschel Walker trade and everyone was excited. The game stuck with Monson, regardless of how poorly the Walker trade worked out.

As PFF grew bit by bit, Monson enjoyed being part of the crew, even if he had no idea where the whole thing was going.

"We had all these different ideas of where it would go; we just had no earthly idea how we were going to get there," Monson said.

When PFF started to gain some traction with the ESPN and the New York Giants deal, Neil approached Monson about grading games and entering the analysis side of things. He was initially unsure about the offer. His reasoning was that participation tracking wasn't too tough and he had other things going on. Monson was playing in a football league and doing some writing on the side. Jumping onboard with grading would mean more time, effort, and most of all, commitment.

After Neil pushed, Monson relented and started grading games. It was a decision that sent him down a career path that he didn't know existed when he chose a history major out of high school. But at first he wasn't sure that he'd found his true calling. PFF was still largely being funded out of Neil's pocket. Monson was making enough money to call it a full-time gig, but it was hardly enough to build a life around.

"All of us were like, 'We want to keep doing this because we believe PFF can become a thing down the road…but do we need to put a stop date on this?'"

He never had to put a stop date on it because as the company grew to prominence, he was its evangelist to the outside world. He started contributing pieces for ESPN as part of PFF's deal, started the *PFF NFL Podcast* with Steve Palazzolo, and got the

PFF Twitter account rolling. When somebody came calling for a guest from PFF to defend any of their opinions on local sports radio shows, it was either Monson or Palazzolo who went on. At times, he was purely a punching bag but the sheer number of people—including within the NFL—who found out about PFF through reading/hearing Monson is incalculable.

One particular incident acted as a shot in the arm to PFF's visibility in the mainstream. In 2014, Monson wrote about how Tom Brady's underlying numbers suggested the legendary quarterback was no longer playing at an elite level. He went in-depth about Brady's decline in accuracy when he was pressured and how the GOAT was struggling when throwing any type of passes that weren't out of his hands quickly.

There's no place as aggressive about sports as Boston and nobody more sacred than Tom Brady. Monson was tossing a hand grenade into a hornet's nest. A Boston.com headline appeared a few days after his article went up with the title, "Idiotic ESPN Report Claims Patriot Tom Brady is No Longer a Top-Five QB in NFL."

The writer, Adam Kaufman, called Monson "a member of Jimmy Garoppolo's fan club" and demanded his readers to not get "bogged down" by numbers.

Boston radio went off. ESPN brought Monson on TV. Every game the following season became a referendum on Monson's take. When Monson said on WEEI radio's morning show the following season that the numbers had improved, Boston TV station NESN noted that he "backtracked" on his take and mocked him with the line, "Just kidding, everyone, Tom Brady is totally an elite quarterback—again."

"Sure, he was wrong ultimately, but you started to see our name pop up in a lot more places…. That accelerated things a lot," Palazzolo said.

"That was my life for a period of time," Monson said. "Going on all of these shows and trying to justify why Tom Brady doesn't have the best PFF grade in the world. And then ironically, right after we write him off in 2014, he goes on this run of being the best-graded quarterback at PFF for five years and is still grading as good as anybody at the age of 43."

Clark, now at The Ringer, pointed out the importance of Sam being willing to stick to his guns in the face of criticism from fans, teams, and local media.

"You saw this in baseball with Bill James, with Nate Silver, with all those guys where, when the data says something, you have to trust it," Clark said. "It's no different than some Wall Street hedge fund guy shorts a stock and it starts to look bad and the hedge fund guy 99 times out of 100 sticks with it and sometimes he's right and sometimes he's wrong. With PFF their ability to trust what their data tells them is really admirable."

Sam indeed has been right way more than wrong over the years, and when he's making his case like he's Tom Cruise in *A Few Good Men,* it's as captivating as any of the world's top sports radio hosts. Everyone had heard of the Colin Cowherds and Jim Romes of the world firing off hot takes, but few people at that time in the football analytics space were bringing confident numbers-based opinions with Sam's vigor.

"I kind of ended up naturally moving to being one of the most front-facing people we have and being the sacrificial lamb to defend the Brady grades and all those kinds of things," Monson said. "Somewhere along the line that developed into an actual job here instead of a side gig from the data collection."

Sam became a master at defending PFF's findings. He would hear the criticisms that PFF didn't know the plays and assignments and therefore its grading system couldn't be taken seriously. He would point out that opposing teams who are studying tape don't know the plays and assignments either. The more of PFF's stances he successfully argued for, the more media spots sports radio wanted him to do. It was even good for PFF when little hit pieces started popping up in which beat reporters would ask players and coaches what they thought of PFF grades and then happily quote them saying that PFF was clueless. But fans either wanted to know more truth from numbers or enjoyed siding with the football men. In either event, it was a must-listen/read when Sam was going against the grain.

One of the football men who took the most vocal anti-PFF stances was Minnesota Vikings head coach Mike Zimmer, who slammed PFF's numbers to the local media in late August 2014. Here's his entire rant:

> The last thing that I want to talk about before I let you guys go is this Pro Football Focus thing. I know everybody wants to get the scoop on this, but quite honestly…. I look at the grades and I can't tell you what a 0.7 is or anything like that, but I know that the people that are grading our games and our defenses and our offenses, they don't know if the tackle gets beat inside, if we weren't sliding out to the nickel or who our guys are supposed to cover. I guarantee they don't know who is in our blitz package and what they are supposed to do. I would just ask everybody to take that with a grain of salt, including our fans. We as coaches get paid a whole bunch of money to do the jobs that we do, evaluate the players that we evaluate and grade them how we grade them and not based on someone else.

Sports Illustrated writer Doug Farrar, who had worked for Football Outsiders previously, called Sam Monson to get a response.

"We would never want anybody taking our grades and stats as the definitive answer to any question," Monson told Farrar. "Football is way too complex for that. But they provide a fantastic starting point and can give you a big shortcut to answers you might be looking for."

Farrar editorialized in the piece in favor of PFF, writing, "I'm a huge fan of what PFF does—they've really sharpened up their writing, analysis, and tape work in the last couple of years, and I have no reservation using their metrics in my own work."

The SI piece opened the door for more understanding of what PFF was doing among fans and media. Their data began to be cited consistently around the same time Sam took on the role as the punching bag. The more local media cited it, the more it inspired questions to coaches and GMs and the more teams wanted to know how PFF was grading its players. Sam's dozens and dozens of radio station appearances and hundreds of articles helped shape the way the up-and-coming generation of football reporters and content creators saw football. He was building on the groundwork set forth by Aaron Schatz at Football Outsiders that normalized analytical writing in football media and using the PFF grading system to run with it. By 2022, the *PFF NFL Podcast* with Monson and Palazzolo ranked on the iTunes charts (per the website Chartable) in the top 15 football podcasts and top 100 sports podcasts.

"It's only when I get messages from my parents or sister now and again when they meet people and they'll be like, 'Wait, Sam Monson is your brother? I love that guy's podcast,'" Monson said. "Or my dad is like, 'Hey, this surgeon that we've got in is a big fan of yours.' And I'm like, I don't know what to do with that but, cool. It's bizarre."

"We started off and everything was behind the scenes and the focus was on the [selling to teams] side.... My interest has always been on the consumer side of things and pushing this out to people and trying to get the net as wide as possible because I always thought that side of things was really valuable. I kind of ended up naturally moving to being one of the most front-facing people we have—and being the sacrificial lamb to defend the Brady grades and all those kinds of things."

The funny thing about Sam Monson and Steve Palazzolo's influence is that they're the ultimate odd couple. Monson is a short(ish) guy from Ireland who didn't know what he wanted to be when he grew up, while Palazzolo is a 6'10" former pro athlete who never wanted to do anything other than play baseball.

Palazzolo went to college at UMass-Lowell. His recruiting trip went like this: "OK, the school looks great, but let's see the baseball stadium." A beautiful place to play, by the way. Palazzolo was at the center of teams that went to the Division II World Series as a freshman and sophomore and had hopes of getting drafted. When he wasn't selected, he didn't want to let the dream die, so he went to play in an independent league in Florence, Kentucky.

From there, the chances of making it into any level of MLB-connected baseball are very slim, but Palazzolo caught enough big-league scouts' eyeballs that he was given an opportunity with the Milwaukee Brewers organization in 2006. He pitched for the Helena Brewers of the rookie league and then the West Virginia Power in Single A.

When that chance didn't materialize, he played Indy ball for another year and then got signed by the San Francisco Giants organization. It was with the Giants where Palazzolo would get within one level of the majors. He pitched very well with the Double A Connecticut Defenders, registering a 3.98 ERA, and got bumped up to Triple A Fresno. That's close enough to smell AT&T Park.

Along his journey through the minors Palazzolo became very interested in anything that could give him an edge as a pitcher, whether it was analytics, nutrition, or mechanics.

"I was my own little—or big—science experiment," Palazzolo said.

The minor league baseball world is taxing on players. Nobody has money except the top draft picks, the bus rides are long, and there's the constant stress of everybody wondering if someday they're going to make it. Palazzolo's outlet to get his mind away from all things baseball was becoming a complete football addict. He became an obsessed *Madden* player, analyzing rosters on the game to make sure they were perfect and printing out depth charts that had everyone's exact position correct. If the game listed a cornerback playing on the outside rather than in the slot, he was going to go in and change it. Back in those days the game didn't have downloadable new rosters on the internet. If a linebacker got traded, Palazzolo had to trade him by hand. And he did.

Ironically, he first found out about Pro Football Focus in 2009 from Boston radio. He was preparing for his first full season in Fresno and the voice on the air was speaking his language by combining the types of numbers he loved in baseball and the game of football that he'd become fanatic about. He started reading game recaps on the PFF website and was captivated by the way in which traditional stats wouldn't match up with PFF's findings. Palazzolo specifically remembers thinking PFF was on to something when its analysis found that New England Patriots linebacker Brandon Spikes had a better game than fellow linebacker Jerrod Mayo, despite a big difference in their total tackles.

When PFF went to a paywall system in 2010, Steve was infuriated. Do you know how many Triple A players can afford to spend $100 on a football website? Not many.

"That was like one-tenth of my monthly salary," Palazzolo said.

Palazzolo emailed PFF to argue his case about why the site shouldn't go behind a paywall. Neil Hornsby replied, and they went back and forth. It wasn't until a year later, when Palazzolo's Triple A career came to an end and he was back in Indy ball, that he reached out to Neil again.

Palazzolo sent a simple email: "Do you need help?"

In response he was sent a game to try doing player participation. Steve was playing for the Southern Maryland Blue Crabs, and fortune would fall his way. The Blue Crabs got rained out for several days in a row, giving him time to do Neil's homework assignment. Neil brought him onboard. He was one of 17 part-timers doing the 2011 season for around $100 a game— gold to an Indy ball player.

Palazzolo's first days on the PFF job were tricky because his baseball season crossed over with the opening of the NFL season.

"I did my first three games during my baseball career while I was still playing," Palazzolo said. "We were finishing our season and we went into the playoffs and on Monday and Tuesday in the locker room the day after [NFL games] I'd have to review these games and do the player participation, so I was doing them in the locker room, I was doing them on hotel WiFi before going to the field, just trying to get NFL Game Pass to work well enough to be able to see the plays."

Going into 2012, Palazzolo was gaining traction at PFF, but he wasn't ready to let go of baseball yet. He prepared through the offseason to play and landed a spot in the Worcester Tornadoes' bullpen. There have been baseball players of yesteryear who have toiled in the minors and Indy ball until they were 30 and then finally gotten their chance, so Palazzolo hoped he would become baseball's next great underdog story. But that wasn't to be. Instead, Jose Canseco took his job.

Canseco, a former major league superstar whose reputation had been sullied by his connection to performance-enhancing drugs, decided that he wanted to come out of retirement and play baseball again. The Tornadoes jumped at the chance to bring in a big-name player who would draw fans to the yard. The rules only allowed four players with pro experience to be on the roster. Palazzolo was the odd man out.

He was happy that his minor league career happened rather than being upset it was over. His now wife was frustrated by the minor league life anyway and told him once that she hoped someday to make him love her more than baseball. He wanted to start a family. He'd already beaten the odds by making it to Triple A and was proud of the way he worked to get past many other players to reach the second-highest level. He learned a lot about professional sports that he has applied along the way and ultimately related to NFL people better than most because of his experience in a competitive environment. But Palazzolo still wonders if maybe, had he mastered the mental part of the game a little better, he could have been playing in big-league stadiums.

"It is a battle of attrition that I think I struggled mentally," Palazzolo said. "A teammate of mine was [major league star] Madison Bumgarner. You see him out there and it's Game 7 of the World Series on two days' rest when I'd be thinking, 'Man, my arm, I don't have my best stuff because of my arm,' and he's just like, 'Whatever, I'm going to throw a slider, I'm going to throw a fastball, what's the pitch, I'm just going to throw it.' I overthought things too much. From a mechanics standpoint, from a how-you-attack-hitters standpoint, if you overthink, you become a completely different player. I think it was consistency and tying that to the mental game."

Many pro athletes search for their identities after the end of their careers. Palazzolo has teammates who still haven't found theirs. They spent their entire lives trying to make it and never thought of anything else. PFF gave Palazzolo his anything else.

In 2012, he learned the grading system—the one that Ben Stockwell and Sam Monson had masterminded through trial and error only a few years before. Palazzolo's work life became about grinding out grades for games, just like he used to grind out a summer road stretch in baseball. He would start at 4 PM ET every Sunday when the first game file arrived and then collect data nearly nonstop through Monday night, putting seven to nine hours into each game. Each game went along with a write-up about its findings, which Palazzolo loved. He was now the guy writing about Brandon Spikes being better in a particular game than Jerrod Mayo. The idea of telling the world about details of the game that were previously uncovered—at least in any type of quantitative way—was thrilling for a former pro athlete who thrived off the details of his previous sport.

Monson and Palazzolo started the podcast around 2013—before everybody had a podcast.

"We didn't really know what we were doing, but whenever we could record we'd talk about stuff and go, much less of a format or consistency to it," Palazzolo said. "But we all had that urge to explain our stuff. I always felt like we needed to prove ourselves. I felt that little brother, we need to prove that what we're doing is good. And I was feeling that…you guys should be using our stats too, you guys should be using our grades too, you guys should be using our stuff to determine All-Pro, you guys should be using our stuff to determine MVP or whatever it might be."

Steve Palazzolo and Sam Monson are quite different in their background and stature, but they became the public faces of PFF.

One of the things that set Palazzolo apart was that he was always looking for ways to talk about PFF's data that pointed to things that teams should be doing. As a former athlete, he was frustrated with football studies that didn't offer solutions. So what if passer rating equates to wins; are we supposed to tell teams to just pass better? He started diving into things like the impact of pressures on quarterbacks and found that pressures were more sustainable from year to year than sack totals, which could be impacted by random spikes based on scheme or luck.

"That's actionable for NFL teams to not overpay for guys with high sack totals and a low PFF pass-rush grade," Palazzolo said.

He also found that the difference in pressure from over the left tackle wasn't all that different from pressure from the right tackle's side, which may have indicated teams were overvaluing the quarterback's "blind side" and overpaying left tackles (or underpaying right tackles).

These were things that hadn't been put in writing or hadn't been studied with the same level of depth because the data for actionable analysis simply wasn't available to use before. Box score stats didn't give an indication of QB pressure. Findings like this started to catch the eye of teams and football fans who were worn out by surface-level football talk. One of Palazzolo's favorite projects was looking into the impact of pressure from different parts of the defensive front at the request of an NFL team.

"We found that Peyton Manning and Tom Brady are both good under pressure, but if you're going to pressure them, do it this way," Palazzolo said. "Manning was really good against interior pressure and Brady was really good against edge pressure. You watch their style and it makes sense. Peyton likes to drift so he can avoid interior pressure, but the edges can get him, where Brady likes to step up in the pocket, so if you have interior pressure, he's in trouble. It's oversimplifying, but I think those are some actionable insights that we've come up with and to me that's the important thing."

Palazzolo's strongest suit was breaking these things down when PFF would meet with teams. He could explain how the grades were gathered, what they could tell coaches and front office members and what they couldn't tell them, and what other data they picked up while grading each game. He knew what pro sports folks were like. He could speak their language and understand what they needed to know.

"There would be defensive coordinators who were like, 'Man, you can give me all these tendencies, when the tight end is off the ball and what they're going to do, run-pass,' that's all they are looking for," Palazzolo said. "They are always looking for data-driven edges from a game planning standpoint. Defensive coaches really loved it."

While he may have known how to talk to football coaches, he also discovered that coaches looked at the game with completely different eyes from analytics enthusiasts. PFF was trying to tell the world who played well and who didn't, but coaches often focused on the raw skills and talents of their players and relied on their own coaching for the rest—the general idea being that they can't teach size or movement, they can teach hand placement or footwork. But that wasn't always true by the numbers. Palazzolo remembers specifically a meeting with then Eagles coach Chip Kelly in which he explained that guard Evan Mathis was a darling of the PFF system because he never took negative grades.

"When [Chip Kelly] is watching a left tackle, he is not quantifying wins and losses; he's looking at traits and knee bend and how well they move and their hands and that's fine," Palazzolo said. "I think we opened his eyes a little bit when we were like, 'We're just looking at wins and losses and how well he blocks the guy and how quickly he blocks them and then on top of that the insights that we drew from that.'"

Not everyone took Palazzolo's explanations as well as Kelly, who eventually became an investor in PFF.

In 2014, Steve was sent to ESPN's campus to give a presentation for former NFL general manager Bill Polian. The former NFL GM had become one of the network's top analysts and PFF hoped to expand its package with ESPN into roles for PFF's personalities and data usage across all of ESPN's platforms. A group of PFFers had met with the ESPN folks, including John Skipper and Jon Gruden, and execs from different areas of the broadcast company beforehand, but Polian hadn't been able to attend and they wanted his opinion. So Steve went back specifically to give Polian a look underneath the hood of what PFF was doing and show him what the company could do for ESPN's football coverage. Polian wanted nothing to do with it from the moment the presentation started. They showed the GM who once drafted Jim Kelly and Peyton Manning their quarterback grades, and he was flummoxed.

"We're showing him our QB grades and if he saw two people out of order, he's like, 'Why is this prospect here, he's terrible,'" Palazzolo said, laughing about his miserable meeting.

Palazzolo tried everything from displaying former players Polian drafted in order to bridge the gap to getting into the nitty gritty of offensive-line play. Nothing budged the old-school GM.

"He's like, 'My wife could tell me that Mike Iupati is a better run-blocker than pass-blocker,'" Palazzolo said. "Everything we do, his wife can do it as well as we can, and he wants no part of this. Previous PFF meetings, at least by the end of it people respected our process. Like, 'I can't believe you have this much information, it's a very unique way of looking at football, some stuff I agree with, some I might not agree, but boy do I respect this process.' I had never been in a meeting where that wasn't at least the vibe, except this one. By the end, Bill was yelling at us."

Neil still grimaces when he talks about the Polian incident.

"That was so far out of kilter from the rest of my experiences with football and football people," Hornsby said. "Everything is in this band of either the most wonderful people on the planet or really nice to you. It's one isolated example of somebody being awful. The one thing that I've been the most shocked at is how this group of tough, macho, hardworking, driven people have been so welcoming and open to us in terms of what we've tried to do."

Put that story in Palazzolo's bucket of surreal moments for a pro baseball player slash *Madden* nut who lost his job to Jose Canseco and never envisioned a career talking about football stats and working directly with NFL teams.

Along with being a front-facing personality, Palazzolo is now a project manager working to grow PFF Ultimate—PFF's one-stop software package that allows coaches and front offices to interrogate the information PFF provides. He works under Rick Drummond to guide the product's growth and improve its effectiveness for teams. His biggest advancement is called "IQ," which pulls in all the PFF data to predict future outcomes for prospects and current players. About a dozen teams are using IQ currently. If they need to know how the new program is actionable, they can still ask Palazzolo, though the sales and team-relationship part of the company has expanded greatly since the days of Neil calling in his big right-hander to explain PFF's process.

Chapter 7

CHANGING HOW
TEAMS OPERATE

B EFORE BRYAN HALL joined Pro Football Focus, he was helping to bring the canning industry into the 21st century.

For the longest time, businesses would make sure they were
meeting FDA canning standards by measuring and writing down
results with pencil and paper. Hall ran North American sales operations for a company that used digital gauges and built software systems to make those tasks more efficient. He would go to companies
like Del Monte and Coca-Cola and sell them on the idea of saving
time and hassle by kicking the old way to the curb. He couldn't have
known how much that would prepare him to be PFF's salesman.

When Hall discovered PFF, he was a massive Green Bay Packers
fan living in Wisconsin. He did what all Green Bay Packers fans
living in Wisconsin do: consume everything Packers. In an online
chat with a Packers beat writer, someone asked the reporter about
sources of statistical information, and he mentioned PFF. Hall
immediately went to the website to see what it was all about and
became a regular reader of articles from people like Ben Stockwell
and Sam Monson.

"I was fascinated by the work they were doing; it just jived
with my mind to quantify performance on the field," Hall said.

One day during the 2011 offseason, Hall saw on the website that PFF was looking for data collectors. He sent them an email and was brought onboard to chart games. The first game took him 15 hours and he thought he might be in over his head, but eventually Hall got into a cadence of working his canning job and then spending his Sundays charting until 4 AM. Once he was comfortable with the process, he started thinking of different ways to spread PFF's word. Hall created an email program to send high-lights of PFF's data to local beat reporters with hopes of increasing the PFF mentions in articles, which he figured would get teams' attention as writers asked questions to coaches and management about the stats. Anyone with ideas to move the company forward also caught Neil Hornsby's attention.

Having a mind for sales, Hall had a vision for what PFF could be in terms of selling to teams. Neil took Hall on in a part-time sales role, and Hall started cold-calling teams.

At first it was tough to get his foot in the door. In 2012, Hall and Neil decided to travel to the NFL combine in Indianapolis in search of selling their data package. Neil flew from the UK and Hall met him in Indy for three team meetings: the Cincinnati Bengals, Carolina Panthers, and Dallas Cowboys. They didn't know where to go, what to wear, or how to entice these teams to buy PFF's data. And because of all that, the first meeting was pretty rocky.

Hall met with his Bengals contact, a tech guy who dabbled in data, inside the Indiana Convention Center. The feedback was not glowing. *Nobody wants this, teams won't want that, here's what you need to do better.* Tough things to hear, but they needed to hear them. The Bengals did not buy what Hall was selling, but he was more prepared for the next meeting. He met with the Carolina Panthers inside a TGI Fridays over beers and appetizers, just like in that epi-sode of *The Office*. The Panthers didn't exactly know how they would implement the data, but they figured there had to be some way to use it, so they bought in. The Cowboys brass is aware that owner Jerry Jones always wants to be ahead of the curve, so they got in too.

Hall and Neil left Indy feeling pretty good about adding two teams to their client list, but they learned something important: they needed to have a product to sell. What they didn't realize going into the meetings was that NFL teams weren't like baseball clubs who had the infrastructure and knowledge to take data and build their own applications in order to use it.

"We were mistakenly assuming that if we just gave them the data, they would figure out what to do from there and they can get it into their system," Hall said. "We figured out pretty quickly that it wasn't that easy."

Hall knew they needed more and would have to invest to gain traction. They hired a Canadian software house to build a platform that took data from all 22 players on the field on a given play and made it searchable and filterable and then linked it to play IDs, which created a picture of the routes and coverages based on charting data. It was called the P.A.T. (Play Analysis Tool) and cost about $100,000.

"It was all of our spare cash," Neil said. "And I do mean all! We had nothing but fumes after that, but it was a strategic gamble that paid off for us massively."

There was still a missing piece: in order to really crack the code, PFF had to link its data to video, which was the lifeblood of NFL teams, and nobody within PFF knew anything about that or how to achieve it.

The answer came in the form of Mike Parker, who called Neil asking if he could get involved. Parker was working for the company XOS Digital, the top video software company for NFL and college teams.

"He was the perfect fit at the perfect time," Neil said. "There was only one problem: I had no money left to pay him."

Parker decided to come onboard anyway.

With Parker's help, they could pair the data and video together.

"We had to refine the format of the data so it could be used by someone other than a math-science guy and could be used by a coach inside their XOS system," Hall said.

Having actual products and Parker's connections with teams got the ball rolling, and PFF started to pick up more teams as clients. Hall used his experience dealing with companies in the canning industry who didn't want to change to understand how to reach teams that felt the systems they already had were good enough.

"I didn't want to just come in and say here's a bunch of data, you wanna buy it?" Hall said. "Here's how I can make your job easier, here's how I can help you find an edge against an opponent. That's how I wanted to come in, but the challenge was that if you came in too hot that way… I've never considered myself a football person; I was a fan. Here's some guy who has never coached who is trying to tell [coaches] what to do. So I had to be cautious about that."

Every team would have people in different roles talk to Hall and Parker. Some teams' interest was on the front office and personnel side, and they wanted to know what they could glean from the grades and data when it came to player evaluation. Others sent the coaching staff, and Hall would explain how the numbers could help

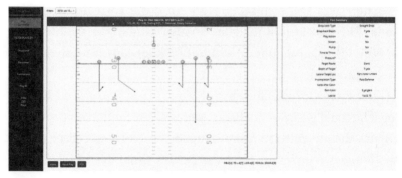

PFF's Play Analysis Tool that draws up X's and O's from data collected is popular among teams.

in the game planning process. For each client they put together an Advance Scout Team that would tailor reports to matchups.

"We would deliver a two-page report that would give bullets of things that looked like tendencies that you might want to explore," Hall said. "It was very passive in a way, because we weren't coming in and telling them, 'This is what you should do.' You give somebody a sheet and, for example, every time they line this player up over here they are running the ball 100 percent of the time. That's something my defensive coordinator is probably going to want to pay attention to. That was the sales process."

Here is an example from the scouting tool showing the accumulation of stats every time the New York Giants used two tight ends and one running back at the same time. It shows which players were used, how often they used this personnel grouping versus down-and-distance, and their success.

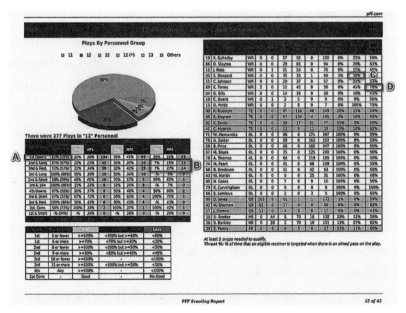

NFL teams use PFF's situational data that is tied to their video. It can show how a team performed in different personnel packages.

Here is an example of how the bullet points would look when presenting the personnel grouping data to a coaching staff:

PFF Offensive Scouting Tool Report

Giants 12 Personnel Tendencies

A. Higher than typical pass tendency out of 12 personnel on 1ˢᵗ Downs (62% pass vs. 45% NFL avg.)
B. Extra TE in 12 personnel usually should help running game, but Giants have struggled running on 2ⁿᵈ Downs. On 2ⁿᵈ & Med only 7% of plays successful vs. 27% NFL avg. On 2ⁿᵈ & Long only 7% of plays successful vs. 15% NFL avg.
C. On pass plays out of 11 personnel, the Giants spread the ball around pretty evenly among the WRs. Out of 12 personnel they're almost twice as likely to target #3 Shephard (38% threat rate) or #89 Toney (41%) than their other WRs (~20%)
D. On Early Downs (1ˢᵗ & 2ⁿᵈ Down, No Garbage Time, No 2min/4min) out of 12 Personnel, #89 Toney is a pass key. The Giants have a 60% pass tendency on Early Downs. That tendency jumps to 78% pass when #89 Toney is on the field.

An example of how Bryan Hall presented PFF's scouting tool to teams.

"Instead of a packet with charts and data, which a coach is going to look at and drop into the garbage because they don't have time to look at it, we tried to deliver a one- or two-page written report with bullet points with very specific ways of using language to not actually report the numbers but instead, what is the gist of this? Why is this valuable to you as a coach? Explain that and then back it up with terms in the bullet point," Hall explained.

"No one is taking out a protractor and calculating probabilities. You're giving a broad tendency to the coach, who is like, 'Oh, I might actually want to pay attention to that.'"

You might be wondering: What does all of this stuff actually mean to coaches? How does it help them be better at football?

"Who the offense has on the field, where they are lined up, and the game situation…these things might give away something that the opponent is doing," Hall said.

"So a coach, for example, can make decisions about what defensive call they are going to use," Hall continued. "Let's say they see a certain player lined up in a certain position and they know from the tendencies shown in the numbers that the offense is going to pass the ball. Well, they can tell their defensive linemen to pin their ears back and charge after the quarterback instead of defending the run."

Just as PFF began picking up momentum with more refined products to show off, one of Hall's early ideas to give stats to beat reporters paid dividends. When Vikings coach Mike Zimmer went on his rant about PFF grading Matt Kalil poorly, Hall contacted Vikings GM Rick Spielman, who was livid about the use of the grading system to criticize his player. To his credit, Spielman was willing to talk it out with Hall and agreed to set up a meeting at the NFL combine. There the team showed Spielman all of PFF's capabilities, and PFF took on the Vikings as a client soon after.

Still, they were aware that they had to tread lightly with the grades. Hall understood that some coaches and front office people couldn't stand the fact that PFF was evaluating their players.

"We'd be like, 'Hey, look; our grades—take 'em or leave 'em,'" Hall said. "Just in your video platform alone we are going to give you 200-plus columns of data that you don't already have. The grades are one or two of those, but if you don't like the grades you don't have to use those columns."

As the company grew, the sales pitch changed. At first Hall was trying to sell teams on things like basic tendencies and the idea that they would be cutting edge and could stay ahead of the competition by buying PFF's data. Once more than half the league bought from them, they sold to clubs who hadn't bought in on the need to catch up—and all the teams eventually did, even the Cincinnati Bengals. Some of the sales were done for Hall by coaches. If a coach went from one team that had PFF's system to another franchise that didn't, they would want PFF's system in their new location, which made for an easy sale.

For the first few years, Bryan split his time between canning and football. He made future plans with hopes for an eventual transition to PFF full time. He used the login "GameChanger" on his laptop for years. He wanted to be part of a company that changed football, and nothing else mattered—not hours, pay, or how demanding Neil could be.

"We're workaholics and perfectionists," Hall said. "We were built as a perfect pipeline for a company because the process and scrutiny and perfection needed to be successful at collecting data naturally [separated] people who were strong in that area and had some of these characteristics that I think jived really well with his leadership."

Splitting time between canning and football created opportunities to pair trips together. Hall went to a canning convention in North Carolina with a number of beer companies and then drove down to the Panthers' facility, walked in the room, and opened a suitcase of beer that he got from the convention. That's one way to get football people on board.

Not all his experiences were as normal as bringing beer to meetings, though. Hall was called in by one particular team and told he would be meeting with the tech people. Instead, the high rollers showed up, including the coaching staff and the team president. They weren't yet using PFF data and grilled him about which other teams were using PFF data to learn about their club. Bryan scrambled to show them the advanced scouting tool and put up the 40-page report on the screen. He left feeling like the meeting hadn't gone particularly well, and the team did not get on board at that time. But later he was told secondhand that it wasn't his presentation or the data that caused them to pass—rather, his slide for the report hadn't used the team name, just the city, and they felt disrespected.

Bryan was able to leave his canning gig in 2014 and begin expanding his sales process to college football teams. It was like starting from square one because the college realm was not familiar with their system or data, but they already knew how to get from Point A to Point B and started vacuuming up college programs.

The structure of sales that was once Hall and Parker mostly doing things the way they saw fit now exists in an entire team of people with multiple sales verticals. There's a group that handles all 32 NFL teams and 132 FBS teams, 40 FCS teams and the XFL, USFL, and CFL. Another vertical is their budding soccer products. Contracts with EA Sports and betting syndicates have their own group, along with agents who pay for PFF reports and television/network deals with NFL Network, NBC, and so forth. All the in-house media—e.g., podcasts, YouTube videos, etc.—has its vertical as well.

This structure didn't arrive at this place easily. Like so many PFFers, Hall's job title and roles morphed many times over the years. He was director of business development and then VP of business development and now he's the chief revenue officer, which involves overseeing all of PFF's sales. Hall and Neil battled over sales and the wages required to compensate an expanding sales group.

"There were some ups and downs, and my position changed over a couple years," Hall said. "One of the things that was tough as a start-up was that it seemed like every year Neil would blow up the system and restart and everyone had new roles…it was really stressful, and I don't think it always served us well."

In recent years, Hall felt unclear about his role and considered leaving PFF to start a brewery, but when his feelings that he was ready to do something else became known, Neil changed course and let Hall build the sales team in his vision as he'd done when he first started at PFF. In 2021 they were named Vendor of the Year by the Collegiate Sports Video Association, an award Hall says is his greatest honor at PFF. The company made around $15 million on the business-to-business side in 2021. When Hall started, that number was about $100,000.

PFF Ultimate is one of the tools that took the football business side of the company to another level and significantly changed the way NFL teams operate.

At the forefront of that project was Rick Drummond.

Before he took me to meet Drummond, Neil and I stood on the rooftop of the Pro Football Focus building. Neil had a big smile on his face. Sweat dripped down into his prickly goatee, and he pointed over to the pro soccer stadium that had recently gone up right around the corner.

"Cool, yeah?"

Neil directed me around to show where the grills and firepits were going to be. Soon enough, the top of the PFF building would be a patio to bring clients and host company parties. It would ultimately become the spot where Neil held his retirement party.

The brick football palace looks like an old firehouse on the outside and inside. You walk in through a large garage, where the grills are being stored in gigantic wooden boxes until it is time to bring them up to the roof, and into a labyrinth of thin hallways, one of which leads to a studio where the PFF personalities record podcasts and go live on YouTube. If somebody dropped you into the studio and you hadn't come from the back corner of downtown Cincinnati and in through the side door of an industrial relic, you would think you were in the NBC studios. Cameras, microphones, lighting, the logo—all top notch. Just three years prior, they were recording podcasts in a closet.

Neil asks a construction worker to remind him how to get back in the building from the roof. He types in the passcode and we enter a maze of offices. Neither Cris Collinsworth nor Neil's space is reflective of two of the most influential people in the football world. Based on number of employees and net worth, PFF now falls under the category of being a mid-sized business. Their offices are similar to that you might find of the guy who runs your local hardware store.

"There's nothing Neil loves more than giving tours of the building," Sam Monson says as we walk by.

We meet Drummond in his office, which is just big enough for him, his desk, and me, and for the door to open without hitting me.

Drummond is an old-school Raiders fan with the outward look of an old-school Raiders fan. His biker goatee ends around his collarbone, and you can picture him putting on spiked shoulder pads and painting his bald head silver and black.

When Drummond was growing up, the Raiders were a force. His dad worked in a candy and tobacco warehouse and bled silver and black. Sometimes Rick's dad would bring home packs of football cards, and nothing was better than reading the statistics and facts on the backs. The Raiders held their training camp in Drummond's hometown of Santa Rosa, so his dad would come home occasionally with stories of running into Raiders players at places where he distributed candy and cigarettes. One day legend Lester Hayes helped unload his truck.

Back when PFF was first starting to publish things to the web, Drummond was looking to settle an argument with a friend about famed Raiders bust draft pick JaMarcus Russell and stumbled upon the PFF website. He landed on Russell's PFF grade, which was predictably terrible, and became intrigued. Drummond started visiting the site regularly and then in 2009 he emailed Neil to ask if there was any way he could participate. For him, PFF was the back of football cards on steroids. Since he wanted to do it, Neil gave him a shot. Neil sent over a game for Drummond to grade: the Steelers–Cardinals Super Bowl.

It was a long road for Drummond to get to the point where he was leading PFF toward its most profound invention.

In the early 2000s, Drummond found himself coaching hockey in Alaska. His former hockey coach's high school–aged son was headed there to play hockey and Drummond agreed to go along to coach and act as the kid's guardian. On the side, he worked at Sears, getting up at 4:30 AM to unload snow-encrusted trucks that had traveled across Canada.

"You lost track of what time of day it was because you're out there in the dark," he said with a growly laugh.

When he returned to Northern California, Drummond became a chiropractor with his own small practice. But three years in, around 2008, the economy took a downturn, his customer base dropped off, and he was forced to close up shop. His wife was in the wine business, so he got into that. Occasionally he would be out in a field doing a sugar test and look around and think about how great it was to get paid to spend time in those beautiful hills. Beautiful views don't pay the bills, though. Around the time he first emailed Neil, he was working in a wine distribution center managing inventory and looking for something to scratch the football itch.

Drummond started grading games and writing summaries for the PFF website. By 2013, he quit working a day job to entirely focus on growing his football career. He was among the Originals to move to Cincinnati from Northern California once Cris Collinsworth bought the company in 2014.

In the years between his first message to Neil and the time the company took a huge step in Cincinnati, he'd grown tight with the group that drove PFF to its biggest pivot point of the Collinsworth purchase.

"When I was in California and these guys were in the UK, we got to be really close because we'd talk every day and we were working toward the same things. We'd know the names of people in their family, but we'd never met their family," Drummond said. "We hadn't sat down and had dinner together, but I'd know the names of their wives and names of their parents."

In that way, the construction of PFF was a sign of the times. In the early 2010s, we started to trust the people we met on the internet. Folks logging on from all over the world to build businesses together was just starting to happen. Years ago, it would have been surprising if you worked for a website with a boss you had never met in person or knew someone who met their spouse while using an online dating service. We wouldn't have trusted a random person from the web to sell us their furniture or show up at our house and give us a ride somewhere, much less employ us. That started to shift with the popularization of message boards, social media, and Skype. The Original PFF team met every day on a Skype call and came to know each other personally as their project grew.

"Especially those guys that were central early on, all of them have introduced kids into this world and we had family tragedies and we had stuff where there were life moments that were big," Drummond said. "To whatever degree, we've been supported, and we've been a side network for everyone."

A quick history of Drummond's jobs at PFF: from 2010 to 2015, he worked as the editor in chief for the PFF site and as an analyst. In 2015, one year after Cris Collinsworth bought the company, he was bumped up to director of football operations and then changed titles from executive director, product management to SVP of football operations. In 2021 he became general manager, football.

During the span of Drummond's employment, PFF's management started to have a problem: as NFL and college teams were starting to use their data more, PFF was taking on heavier loads of inquiries. Building statistical models ad hoc in Excel sheets and then sending them via Dropbox was not an efficient model.

"It was a very immature way of doing things," Drummond said.

They set out to bring everything under one roof. To create tools that teams' analytics departments could use themselves to get answers with a few mouse clicks rather than having to ask PFF's data analysts every time they needed something.

"When we went out to teams in the early days, we sold them data and we would go back to them a year later and say, 'Did you get anything out of it?'" Neil said. "It became apparent that they didn't know what to do with it."

In 2017, Drummond led a group that gathered in Neil's basement to hash out exactly how it would work. PFF Ultimate came to life.

One of the most important elements of getting Ultimate up and running was Neil's PAT tool, which did play diagramming. Drummond's group created a system by which teams could search specific plays and instantly get the diagram and video clip of the play. Let's say you wanted to see all the touchdowns Aaron Rodgers threw last season. *Click, click, boom.* You could see them in an instant, along with every statistic imaginable from those plays.

"And that's what made it catch," Drummond said. "That made it land right. [Teams would say], 'Oh, I can see you have the clips and how this would be useful.'"

Drummond starts running down all the possibilities of search inquiries. Do you want to see the depth that a quarterback dropped back on fourth-quarter passes and all the statistics from all those throws? Do you want to see the coverage that an opponent used on every third down? How about run schemes on second-and-10?

"It's a report of stats that looks like a report of stats on any website you'll ever see," Drummond said. "It's a table of names and numbers but we can take it from there and make it into other things, as long as we start with the piece that isn't scary. We don't want people to open it up and turn it off right away or go, 'What the fuck is this?'"

By 2019, PFF Ultimate was on the computers of all 32 teams.

How is it helping them? You can imagine how fun it would be to toy with all the different numbers—like bringing the backs of baseball cards to life—but how does that increase the chances of a team winning football games?

Drummond explained that teams have been doing studies since the beginning of time in football, but the process was painstaking. An assistant coach would be assigned to look at a specific element of their team or an opponent's games for some purpose. For example, if a team was playing the Packers and they were trying to scheme against Rodgers' air attack in the red zone, a coach would need to sift through hours of game tape looking for those Rodgers red zone throws and then try to figure out what the Packers have been doing to get receivers open. With PFF Ultimate, it's gathered instantly there in front of them with a simple search. It took Jon Berger's process of looking at player participation and pulling clips himself and brought the two together, only with much more data.

"You no longer have to watch 1,000 snaps of this guy playing during the season to find the 15 snaps you're interested in," Drummond said.

"It's really just a couple of steps," he continued. "Shape the filters, shape the data set and the set of plays that I'm interested in, and get a report showing a set of plays and then within that report I'm looking at that report or that guy broken down by game or by season.... If I want to see that there's X number of passes that have gone for first downs in this situation or I want to see what they did on the plays, that gets them to the [film] cut-ups. So they can get to the video and digest it the way they would have digested it for the last 40 years, but they got there in a snap of the fingers rather than having to work on piecing it together."

Rick Drummond headed up PFF's game-changing product called
Ultimate, which is used by every NFL team.

Oftentimes when football fans hear about analytics, it's from
broadcasters talking about whether they attempted a fourth down
or went for two. Teams definitely use analytics for those decisions,
but 95 percent of data usage can't be spotted by watching on TV.

"Coaches are in a permanent crunch," Drummond said.
"There's a currency that develops in all of that. The minutes and
the hours that they're spending. You can take a task and make it
from a five-hour thing to a five-minute thing. It's super valuable
because you're not only getting them to their answers faster, [but]
helping them open up time to do more or to spend more time
coaching or spend more time doing the stuff that they want to be
delivered in that information. If we walked into a team that we

weren't working with and we could say only one thing to them, that's what it is."

What PFF said with Ultimate is: we can help you capture the numbers *and* the film and simply do the same job in a sharper way.

"We believe we can help in their efficiency, allowing them to be even better," Drummond said. "There's 32 people on the planet who end up with an NFL head coaching job and you're one of them—you're obviously good at something; we can help you be even better at it if you want us to."

Just because it makes sense doesn't mean everyone is going to get it. But Drummond has a special ability to play translator between the data and coaches.

"The biggest issue in business…is the ability of somebody to be able to connect the user to the IT person," Hornsby said. "A person who's smart enough to be able to talk football at the level of a head coach and talk IT at the level of an IT professional. Normally, if you have a head coach and IT professional, nobody would know what the other person was saying. It would be like one person would be speaking Chinese and the other person speaking Dutch. That translation role is what you need in every business and every project like that. Drummond just fell into it so brilliantly."

Of course, Drummond being the go-between comes with its challenges, like the time one team wanted a particular shade of blue for the tight ends. So he created an option for teams to color the positions whatever way they pleased. That data being customizable was actually vital to the process. Not exactly the part about the color, but PFF didn't have the manpower to handle requests for reports all year long. They needed the teams to be able to do it themselves.

"You need to have one version you give to everybody," Hornsby said. "Don't have a different version for the Jets as you do for Seattle. If you do that, you're sunk. If you put out something that needs to go to all of them, you need one version of the software. Teams wanted to do their own things and be proprietary. We needed to build a report builder. It sounds easy, but it's really difficult."

Making that process happen was the linchpin to getting teams to use it on a consistent basis, which PFF tracked through the keystrokes in the program.

At the 2022 NFL Combine, Drummond and his team met with teams and went through some of the latest features of Ultimate. Neil was floored.

"I was sitting there watching them go through it and I said to Drummond, 'What you've done with my fucking hairbrained idea is unbelievable,'" Hornsby said. "Even in the last six months, all of this stuff that's in there, it was all tremendous and all well beyond my capacity for understanding."

During our conversation, even the tough-looking Drummond couldn't help but be reflective about Ultimate.

"Bringing this thing to life was my contribution to the football world," he said.

It wasn't long ago that he felt embarrassed over his failed chiropractic practice. It wasn't that long ago he was talking over a move from Northern California to Cincinnati with his wife and wondering if they would be able to adjust to a new life. He thinks about how he put his trust in a stranger from England whom he came to know on a deeply personal level over years of phone calls and Skype chats. And he looks around sometimes and wonders what he did to deserve his dream job.

"A lot of this is because Neil set a tone early on," Drummond said. "Even in the muddiest moments we've had along the way, he's had clarity. He's a good rock to have."

Before I left his office, Drummond wanted to make it clear that he wasn't taking his victory lap or waving to the crowd.

"We've still got a long way to go," the Raider-at-heart said.

But here's how far data usage has come in football in a short time: when the New York Giants first contacted Neil, they were only looking for information about which players were on the field for all the teams. That wasn't even 10 years prior to PFF Ultimate's launch.

Chapter 8

THE ACQUISITION

S ITTING ON OPPOSITE SIDES of the backyard patio table on a hot summer evening, Neil and Claire talk about how differently they experienced one of the most important moments of their lives.

Claire remembers how quickly everything changed. In June 2014, Neil was closing in on a deal to sell Pro Football Focus to Cris Collinsworth. They flew from England to Cincinnati. Neil was going to meet with Collinsworth and his investors, and Claire was asked to have a look around with Cris' wife, Holly, and figure out if she'd be happy with raising their family in Ohio.

"I fell in love in those three days," Claire said.

Cincinnati offered more space than they had in the UK, and she felt that their two middle school–aged boys would thrive. They only needed to look at a single house and she was sold. But there were so many steps that needed to be taken for Pro Football Focus to belong to Cris and for the Hornsbys to become Americans. They put an offer on the house before their visas had been approved.

"I remember saying to Neil, 'This could be a very expensive holiday home if this doesn't work out,'" Claire said in her naturally calm voice. "But we just had the conversation that we just have to assume everything is going to work out. We have to be in this with both feet and not look back. Pretty much that's how we did it."

The euphoria was followed by some tough days for Claire. Neil stayed in Cincinnati during the fall and Claire was left feeling in the dark, only sensing from tense phone conversations with Neil that everything wasn't going swimmingly. She was busy trying to close out their lives in the UK and prepare to open new ones in America. Anyone who has even moved across town knows how many more boxes need to be checked than you ever expect. Imagine bringing a family across the pond. She was also acting as the company's finance director at the time and was being asked to dig up all sorts of information.

"The lawyers were treating it like a big corporate acquisition, and I was saying, 'It's just Neil in the back bedroom, we don't have a vault of files," Claire said.

She was booking tutors to prepare the boys for American schooling. Ethan, who was in ninth grade, was hesitant about the change. He made a list of 18 demands, and he would only move to the U.S. if they were met.

Neil remembers trying to shield Claire and the Originals from the stress and pressure he was feeling.

"It was horrendous," Neil said. "It was by far the most stressful time of my entire life. That whole acquisition process drove me insane. Probably to tears on more than one occasion."

The Hornsbys' life was thrown into a state of excited disarray when Collinsworth contacted PFF about using some of their data and then began a dialogue with Neil that took them down a rabbit hole that led to the legendary football broadcaster buying the company. Neil had been poking around options to sell PFF because he understood that they wouldn't be able to grow without a major investment and wouldn't be able to keep the Originals around if he continued paying them at their current rates.

When Collinsworth and his investors agreed to buy the company for $6 million, Neil felt like they were at the 1-yard line, just needing to hash out the details before changing everyone's lives. It turned out that they were much farther away from the end zone—more like the parking lot at best. Neil's lawyer was in the UK, and his price tag wasn't cheap. The meter was running and months into the negotiation, Neil owed about as much in legal fees as PFF would make in yearly profits.

"It was unbelievably stressful because of all the hopes and dreams that you're holding for virtually everybody," Neil said.

About two months after the original agreement, Neil was on his way to a preseason game in Detroit when he got a phone call from Collinsworth. He was told the deal was off.

The lawyers were concerned that the NFL was going to have PFF shut down over the usage of the league's properties and that Cris and his investors would be throwing their money down the toilet. Simply put: they were very concerned that Neil never had the right to use their broadcasts to create his system and sell his products in the first place.

Neil knew that wasn't right because of fair use, but he couldn't convince them, and fair use is not a black-and-white law. He sat, distraught, in the press box in Detroit, thinking about all the people he'd be letting down if this deal didn't go through. He didn't want to tell anyone what was happening. The Originals had no idea what was going on. Claire had only a vague feeling based on Neil's stress level.

"That whole sense of them being so close to their dreams and me being the root cause of it not coming to fruition—if the deal hadn't come off, I know deep in my heart of hearts we would have regrouped…but my god, would it have been hard and at that particular time just at that moment, I thought, 'I just want to quit. If this doesn't go through, I just want to quit. I just can't go through this,'" Neil said.

On a Sunday in August, Neil sat in Collinsworth's house practically begging him to understand that they were allowed to produce the data.

"If it's broadcast, anyone has a right to make any comments they want on that performance and you can do anything you want with it," Neil argued.

But Collinsworth and his investors still couldn't go forward with the lawyers saying it was too risky. Collinsworth wanted to talk to another lawyer who might understand the topic better. Monday went by, nothing. Tuesday, nothing. Wednesday, nothing.

"I had this horrible view that [Claire and the boys] were going to come across, they were going to land, and this whole thing was going to be off," Neil said. "I just felt that I was letting so many people down."

On Thursday, a lawyer who had worked with the NFL confirmed to Collinsworth that PFF wasn't breaking any rules and the acquisition could go forward.

Neil finally got to make the phone calls that he'd fantasized about for months telling the team that the deal was final. The shares that he once said wouldn't be worth the paper they were printed on were now worth thousands. Ben Stockwell had thought so little of his share when he got it that he couldn't find it in his house. He had to fill out special paperwork to get his money.

"Some of the guys, when I told them how much money they were going to get with their shares, they were literally in tears," Neil said. "One of the guys told me that it saved his marriage. Other guys couldn't believe it; they were over the moon."

Neil felt the weight of the world lift off his shoulders.

"I think that's the pressure you put on yourself and you always do when you imagine having the ability to give somebody something that will make them happy," Claire said. "For Neil, he wanted to give us a nicer lifestyle, but he really wanted to make sure all these people were taken care of."

Neil Hornsby sold PFF to Cris
Collinsworth in 2014.

"I just felt a huge amount of responsibility…more for the guys who were working for us, because we had a reasonable life anyway," Neil said. "For some of those guys, this was a huge opportunity for them to do something they loved…this opportunity probably wouldn't have come along many times in a lifetime. The main reason we were here is because of them—because of the work that they had done."

There were still a few more hoops to jump through before the deal could be completed, including tracking down everyone who had shares. There were a handful of people who had come and gone, and they needed to get what they were owed.

Neil and Claire both shook their heads and laughed in amazement as the sun went down telling the story of one such person who couldn't be found because he was in the hospital with serious injuries.

"I finally get through to him and I'm telling him the story and he's telling me what's happening to him…he's been in a car crash and he hasn't been able to use a computer because he's only just getting back the use of his arms and legs," Neil said. "I'm feeling sorry for him and all this…. I'm telling him about the deal and I'm really happy that we're getting the deal done and he's incredibly happy about it. This is going to cover his hospital expenses and I'm just starting to tear up."

The first step Neil wanted to take was getting his people paid properly. Some went from getting nothing to making $60,000 per year. They began the process of moving key members to the new headquarters in Cincinnati and Neil, Claire, and their two boys, Ethan and Alex, started their new life there as well.

Neighbors were fascinated with their accents and intrigued about why they had come from England. The dog escaped the yard from time to time, forcing them to go out into the neighborhood and meet people. Ethan's demand list was met to his liking. Alex joined the wrestling team and started making friends, eventually going on to help as an assistant coach after he was done with high school.

"When I go down and see the office, I'll say to Neil, 'Gosh, I remember when you were in our back bedroom in our little house in Luton and now look at this. You must be so proud,'" Claire said. "To provide that much work for people and work that they really enjoy."

Neil points out that all the Originals who got the share payouts at the time of the sale are still working at PFF seven years later.

One of the key members of PFF who bridged the gap between Neil and Cris Collinsworth and PFF and the teams was Mike Parker.

Parker played college football at the University of Kentucky, where he was the backup for famed college quarterback Jared Lorenzen. When I first visited PFF in 2018, everyone was taking turns trying to throw a football through a hole in a 10-foot board that was set up in the garage area. From about 25 feet back, nobody could make it. Parker stepped up and nailed it on the second throw. Even the Kentucky No. 2 QB is better at football than anyone you know.

When Parker finished his college football career he wanted to become a coach. He worked as a graduate assistant at Kentucky and coached high school but didn't gain traction in the coaching realm in the way he had planned. Through his time coaching, Mike built a relationship with the video company XOS (now called Catapult), which offered him a job to work with its college and NFL team customers.

What XOS is and how it came to be requires a bit of a history lesson. See, back in the old days of the NFL, coaches would say, 'We gotta watch the film,' because it was literally film. In order to look at a group of plays, someone had to physically cut actual film and splice it together. In 1986, the NFL went to using cassette tapes and coaches started saying, 'We gotta watch the tape.' By the mid-90s, digital companies started popping up. Avid Sports was the first to start selling to teams when it created a system to copy the Betamax tape and digitize it so coaches could easily cut it up.

Digital made it a zillion times easier to exchange as well. Teams at the college and pro level used to be required to give upcoming opponents their game film. That was a painstaking process.

"In the old days, you'd have to send all of your game film out to be developed and it would take some time and you'd get it the next day and then you'd have to send your reels to your opponent and that would take a couple days...so your game from Saturday, I might not get until Tuesday or Wednesday," Parker explained. "With tape things got faster; you didn't have to send it out to get developed by some photography group, so you'd get it the same day, but you'd have to exchange everything through the airplane. We drive down to the airport, and we pick up the other one, so everything had to be really slow."

Once the video was digital, it could be exchanged instantly. Everyone in football quickly bought into the digital video way. A company called Pinnacle bought Avid Sports and then XOS launched soon after that. XOS bought Pinnacle and owned a near monopoly over college and pro sports video at the time it hired Mike Parker.

For a number of years, Parker's job was to work with teams on their XOS systems, helping with updates, improvements, and any issues they were having. In 2011, XOS formed a partnership with a data company called STATS Inc. and the plan was to link all the video to STATS Inc.'s data. After quite a bit of effort, XOS was able to tie the video with the numbers and teams began using it. But it wasn't quite everything they were looking for. Parker talked with Mike Stoeber, a former XOS employee who had been hired by the Jacksonville Jaguars, about the system, and Stoeber told him that it was "OK," but that the Jags preferred the Pro Football Focus data. That was the first Parker had heard of PFF.

In 2013, Parker was visiting the New York Giants, where Jon Berger—the same Jon Berger who had first reached out to Neil Hornsby about using PFF's data—told Parker that he was frustrated by the fact that the Giants had to take PFF's numbers and then have someone hunt down the plays on video that they connected with. Say, for example, the Giants coaching staff noticed via the PFF data that Tom Brady had amazing numbers with a fullback on the field. They would have to have someone look through hours of tape to find all the plays with a fullback on the field in order to analyze them. Parker wondered if PFF could use somebody like him to put the data and film together.

Parker had a similar experience in Oakland. The Raiders' statistical analyst, George Li, stopped Parker in the hallway during a visit with the team's coaching staff and said that he had been told there was a way to connect the two vital entities.

"I showed him the limitations and he was super disappointed," Parker said. "I kept that in the back of my mind, and I was starting to have these types of conversations more and more."

Parker asked Jon Berger to put him in touch with PFF and he ended up on the phone with Neil. They talked for weeks about ideas and ways that Parker could potentially help them take the next big step in selling to teams. The problem was that Neil didn't have the budget to add another person. But hypothetically, if they sold more to teams, there would be money to pay him.

On Halloween 2013, Parker left his job at XOS to take an unpaid position with PFF out of sheer belief in what Neil was doing. He got to work right away with Ian Perks building systems that could combine the XOS video with the PFF data. Parker used his relationships with teams to get the ball rolling quickly. It wasn't long after that they had connected with a significant chunk of the league.

He remembers a meeting with one old-school defensive line coach in which the coach threw his phone against the wall out of frustration. When Parker asked what was wrong, the coach said that he knew that everything about the way coaches operated was about to change.

"When I first joined up with PFF and we were looking at this, we'd sit down with a team and you'd see at some point that the light turns on and they're like, 'Oh, I get it now,'" Parker said. "Teams would think we were going to come in there and tell them to go for it on fourth down or when to kick a field goal, and then they found out we were actually going to make their jobs easier."

But things didn't change instantly. Parker worked for PFF for nine months before seeing a paycheck.

"On the surface it looks nuts, but we survived. It was tight, but we survived," Parker said. "I really believed in what we were doing. Looking back on it, it sounds risky, but to me it wasn't risky because I knew that it would work."

It wasn't long after Parker joined PFF that he and a dozen other PFFers were on a Skype call with Neil when their leader announced something that caught everyone's attention: Cris Collinsworth had reached out to Neil. Timing and coincidence have played into many things regarding PFF's success, and Parker's role is no different. Parker lived about 10 minutes away from Collinsworth. He offered to show Collinsworth what they were doing, and they set up a meeting.

"I think Cris was blown away by the fact that he had no idea what teams had at their fingertips," Parker said. "He was in this world of preparation and watching from play one to the end and I can't break it down into pieces if I just want to see Tom Brady in the end zone. I think it opened his eyes to the business."

Parker participated in the negotiation process so the team could show Collinsworth the breadth of PFF's capabilities.

"If we weren't selling to teams, I don't know if he buys it or he's interested in buying it; he's probably just an advocate," Parker said. "That's what I'm most proud of, the role that I played in helping PFF become a legitimate business that worked on the team side."

Finally, Parker got paid when Collinsworth bought the company. The service department has expanded from being Parker and Parker alone to about a dozen people. As PFF builds more products for teams to use, Parker's group makes sure they are being implemented inside NFL and college buildings and that teams know how to use them.

Every so often, Parker gets an offer from an NFL team to leave PFF. Sometimes it's for much more money than he's making now, but he's never had any reason to leave.

"I don't expect anyone to understand it," Parker said. "I think it was Lou Holtz that said when someone asked what it was like at Notre Dame, 'If you've been here, no explanation is necessary, and if you haven't, no explanation is satisfactory.' There's a side of that that a lot of people who have been in the company a long time would resonate with."

Chapter 9

CRIS COLLINSWORTH

O NE OF THE FIRST THINGS people ask about Cris Collinsworth's ownership stake in Pro Football Focus is whether he's *actually* involved with its operation.

Crammed into the corner of a downtown Cincinnati cafe, the former NFL star and broadcaster makes that answer very clear by the concern in his voice.

It so happens that I picked an interesting time in PFF's history to talk to Collinsworth. In July 2021, he and Neil Hornsby were deep in negotiations to sell a 30 percent stake in the company to the private equity firm Silver Lake. PFF was given a valuation of $160 million, so bringing Silver Lake into the mix would not only mean a cash windfall but it would give them an opportunity to add many more employees and build entire new wings for other sports, like soccer. But Collinsworth was worried that getting into business with a private equity firm could have unintended consequences.

"I've talked to a lot of people about taking money from private equity and relinquishing control and some of the horror stories that go with that," Collinsworth said in a nervous cadence TV viewers wouldn't recognize. "They're going to try to build it up and sell it. That has not been my goal. That has not been Neil's goal. Our goal is that we are trying to change the football world."

A former NFL player and NBC broadcaster, Cris Collinsworth bought Pro Football Focus in 2014.

Collinsworth talks about the medical care industry and the ways in which private equity firms cut from hospitals and made them less safe. He says he read an entire book about it. Collinsworth talks about friends that he's known who took big cash payouts and then found their companies unrecognizable a few years later.

"I want to have a family business," he said. "I want for my kids to work there. I'd much rather give them a company than give them money. They're built for it. Austin has a finance degree and MBA from Notre Dame. My daughter went to Harvard. They're built for it. But I don't think that will be what motivates Silver Lake."

Collinsworth said he was comfortable working with Silver Lake and the people he was directly negotiating with and felt they had a shared vision for the future of the company, but he was worried about the idea that they could bring in more investors from the outside and hand those people decision-making power.

"I do not want them to have veto power over us," Collinsworth said, resolutely. "As much as I want this to work out, I can't sign that and I won't sign that. Neil and I don't butt heads very often, but he thinks what they are asking for is fine and I'm probably on the other side, but I'm not risking it."

Weeks later, the agreement went through without Collinsworth having to sign away his soul and he was able to go back to eating his lunches across from the PFF offices with less stress. He still has 46 percent of the company and remains the chairman.

"Cris had every lawyer in the country going over this thing," Hornsby said, laughing. "And at the end of the day they maybe got a few minor concessions."

Collinsworth's apprehension about doing anything that could put the future of PFF in jeopardy is emblematic of how close PFF is to his heart and how much he went through to turn a $6 million buy into a $160 million company.

Only seven years before the deal with Silver Lake was signed, Collinsworth had never heard of PFF.

The 16-time Emmy winner discovered Hornsby's invention when he was poking around the internet for a website that would give him recaps of all the NFL games. He'd been offered extra duties by NBC, so he was hoping for a go-to place to get the "down and dirty" breakdown.

Pro Football Focus came up in a Google search and Collinsworth started clicking around. He got out his credit card, paid the $26.99 subscription fee, and was taken aback by the available information.

It was nothing like the traditional box scores he'd been looking at for his entire football life.

"I'm starting to see these color-coded depth charts, and I had just done six of these teams and I knew what the coaches thought and I knew what my film study thought and I had real detail on some of the teams, so I'm going down and I'm like, 'Damn, this is pretty dead on,'" Collinsworth said.

As the son of two educators, Collinsworth is a naturally curious man. When he found a whole new world of football numbers, he needed to know more. What brilliant football mind is behind PFF? So he went to the "Contact Us" section of PFF's site and sent a message that read, more or less, "Who the heck are you guys?"

Collinsworth's phone rang seconds later. It was Neil. When Collinsworth heard Neil's British accent, he thought he'd been ripped off. No matter how much money you've made in your life, nobody wants to have $26.99 stolen from them by some internet scam. He was mad. He was expecting a former football player or coach and the guy talking to him was the farthest thing from that.

Collinsworth started firing football questions at Neil and quickly changed his tune.

"This guy knows way more about the league than I know," Collinsworth said. "This is unbelievable what he's doing here. I asked him, 'Who are you?' I'm like, he's an alien or something, you know? He starts telling me the story of PFF and I'm like, 'Oh my god, that's unbelievable.' Somehow it turned into partnering with him and somehow we got around to, would I be interested in buying the company?"

Collinsworth didn't know what he had stumbled upon exactly, but he knew he didn't want anybody else to have it. Without even running it past his wife, Collinsworth jumped in headfirst.

"I had no idea what I was doing, none," Collinsworth said. "Neil Hornsby could have taken that money and gone to the mountains in the Swiss Alps."

A slide from Neil Hornsby's presentation to sell the company to Cris Collinsworth.

Collinsworth started to feel better about his purchase almost immediately. Well, aside from the part about not telling his wife, Holly. He says she's still unhappy about that.

Collinsworth brought on former Cincinnati Bell CEO Jack Cassidy. One night they met with Dave Calhoun, who is the president and CEO of Boeing, to talk about the investment. Collinsworth thought the decorated businessman was going to tell him that he was making a huge mistake, but Calhoun felt otherwise. He had once been at the forefront of Nielsen Holdings (responsible for Nielsen ratings) growing into a billion-dollar company and saw PFF's data as a major find.

"I'm explaining this thing the best I can and [Calhoun] goes, 'Cris, can I talk to you for a minute outside?' I was like, 'Oh god, he's going to tell me this is the dumbest thing you've ever done.' And he pulls me out there and he goes, 'Cris, I can't tell you how much like Nielsen this is. If you had ever told me my television ratings would have something to do with where Coca-Cola is placed in a grocery store, I would have told you that you're out of your mind. It's all about the data. It's only about the data. Once you own the data, you're going to find a bunch of MIT and Harvard guys who know what to do with it, but you just protect the data… you just do everything you can to make it ironclad and I think you've got a billion-dollar business.' I went, '*WHAT?*'"

Calhoun came on as an investor at $2.5 million.

At the beginning of Collinsworth's tenure, things were tough as he adapted to the life of a businessman. Collinsworth learned the hard way about a concept called the "Hockey Stick," which essentially says that when you start a new business, your money goes down before it can start going up.

Neil wanted to make sure that the crew that had built the foundation of Pro Football Focus was rewarded for all the hours that they had put in for little or no pay. He also wanted to retain them and entice them to move to Cincinnati, as well. So part of the deal was giving raises to the group that had spent their nights grinding out player participation tracking and grading for years. They also needed to hire people if they wanted to take big steps forward.

PFF Valuation - EBITDA Model

Company	Item	2012	2013	2014	2015
PFF	Revenue	$ 250,881.00	$ 617,000.00	$ 975,200.00	$ 1,717,300.00
PFF	Costs	$ -	$ 490,000.00	$ 630,000.00	$ 680,000.00
CFF	Revenue	$ -	$ -	$ 60,000.00	$ 350,000.00
CFF	Costs	$ -	$ -	$ -	$ 150,000.00
Revenue		$ 250,881.00	$ 617,000.00	$ 1,035,200.00	$ 2,067,300.00
7 x Revenue		$ 1,756,167.00	$ 4,319,000.00	$ 7,246,400.00	$ 14,471,100.00

On a model used for valuing start-up companies (7 times Revenue) PFF should be valued at a minimum of $7.25 Million. This however neglects a number of important factors.

PFF's valuation before the company was sold to Cris Collinsworth.

"When you're spending your own money and you really don't know what you're doing—which I really didn't—and you're trying to explain this hockey stick to your wife, it gets complex," Collinsworth said. "The other thing is, now I'm hiring a bunch of people and I don't know if I'm going to make payroll for the month now. It was a really intimidating, scary time. But anybody who's ever started a business will tell you the exact same thing."

In the early days of Collinsworth's leadership, there was major progress. He was dead set on applying all the principles of the NFL data to college football. He believed that was the biggest area in which the company could grow. Neil and his crew got to work right away on making the college vertical happen. They aimed to grade every college game by the end of the college season—which was a ridiculous task with a group of graders who had only previously been asked to cover 16 NFL games a week. It came down to the wire and the final month before the deadline is still remembered as "Hell Month," but the graders got it done and PFF's college coverage was born. Now PFF has more than 120 college team clients. NFL teams were also very interested in college data because of the draft. They had very little to work with outside of scouting before PFF took on the college project.

Cris also believed in changing the grading system from a plus-minus to a 1–100 system. Why? Because he felt that players of the insanely popular *Madden* video game series would relate more to ratings on that scale. Could you tell another person that Linebacker X was a plus-16.7 and have them know what it meant? No, but you could tell them the linebacker had a 90.5 grade out of 100 and they'd get it instantly.

"My kids pushed me so hard to put it to a 1–100 grade," Collinsworth said. "'Dad, you're trying to sell this thing to my generation.' They know *Madden*. They know the *Madden* grades. They know what that means. I wasn't very popular on that one."

Soon after, PFF grades started showing up on the *Sunday Night Football* broadcast as player rankings. That wasn't Collinsworth's doing. Legendary producer Fred Gaudelli was behind that.

"He said it was a powerful thing both positively and negatively, to say this guy is No. 2 of 100 players or this guy is No. 99 of 100 players," Collinsworth said of the move that helped increase PFF's national reach.

Neil was fine with changing the grading system that he had invented and that Ben Stockwell had refined. Some people felt that it didn't truly capture how much better one player was than the next. The great 1–100 debates raged on, in part because PFF couldn't find a good way on the *Madden* scale to truly convey how good J.J. Watt had been during those years. Watt was so far ahead of everyone else on the plus-minus scale that he would have needed to be a 110 in order to have the next-best defensive tackle be rated in the 90s.

But the grading scale issue helped Collinsworth learn a valuable lesson about decision-making. With new people coming into the company, PFF was having meetings upon meetings trying to decide which direction to go on a number of important issues. Eventually Collinsworth threw up his hands and made an important change: he and Neil were going to make all the decisions. No more spending weeks and weeks meeting over one particular issue and spinning their wheels. Like a wide receiver running a route, he knew they needed to pick directions and go.

"I completely changed how I did it. I said, 'Neil, you and I are going to decide everything,'" Collinsworth said. "It doesn't mean that we're the expert on everything and we would take a lot of input from as many people as we could, but the decisions would come from me and Neil sitting down in a room together and deciding. What we finally figured out was: our greatest advantage was that by the time big companies can come to a decision on anything, they've been through the process that we've been going through. It took them six months to a year just to make a decision."

"The really hard decisions in life are usually 50-50 calls, so why are we stressing ourselves to death trying to decide a 50-50 call? That's impossible. Presidents can't do that. You have to go. Make a choice and go. If I have to say the one big breakthrough, the one big thing that I think changed our company forever, it's that. We got out of the committee meetings and Neil and I just started making decisions as fast as we could make them. Did we get them all right? No. But we got enough right."

When Collinsworth first bought PFF, he named Jack Cassidy CEO. It became clear that it wasn't a fit.

"Jack was trying to turn us into a corporation because that's how Jack knew to manage businesses because he was a corporate CEO," Hornsby said. "It frustrated Cris and it frustrated me, and we never seemed to get much done very quickly."

It wasn't long before tension built and Cassidy handed in his resignation, expecting Collinsworth to reject it and work things out. Instead, Collinsworth accepted it.

They looked at other potential CEOs and interviewed one businessman whose claim to fame was making money for investment firms. Neil looked at his résumé and realized that most of those businesses didn't exist anymore. He told Cris that he wasn't going to continue with the company he'd founded if they named another corporate CEO. He wanted to continue to quarterback PFF even if he didn't own it anymore.

"It felt like a follow-me-or-trade-me type of thing," Hornsby said. "Cris said, 'There's no way I'm letting you go. There's just no way.'"

Collinsworth named Neil the CEO. Cassidy sold his shares at a $50 million valuation.

Things took off from there. College, NFL draft, social media, gambling, fantasy, data science, the pursuit of getting all 32 teams on board and then building a mega system that had never been seen before in professional sports.

"Since Cris Collinsworth has been in charge—if you track PFF's success and you can do this in terms of value and you can see when Cris Collinsworth took over and he was the only person who was in charge of this business, it just goes like that [points straight up], it's like a skyrocket," Hornsby said.

Collinsworth could have backed away and left PFF to more experienced businesspeople to take the reins. So why did he go through those difficult times in the early days to set the company on its current path?

"One of the things that people don't realize because he's such a nice guy is what a competitor he really is and how much he wants to compete," Hornsby said. "He didn't want people disrespecting him and patronizing him. It felt like Jack was patting him on the head, like, 'You're a football player; what the fuck would you know about business?' Jack never said that in as many words, but he might as well have at times. What [the Silver Lake deal] does for Cris is that it says, look, this company has, since Jack left and sold his shares, gone up $110 million in valuation. I'm really pleased for Cris."

The other part of Collinsworth taking the path of more resistance to keep building PFF is his sheer fascination with football and the buzz he gets from spending endless hours looking for the right answers.

"When you have a boss like Cris who is in it for the long term and he's trying to build a great, enduring company, then you can focus on things that are important to people in the long term and you know will have great value. It's not about making more money for 'the man' and enforcing shitty rules and regulations from somebody who probably doesn't know their ass from their elbow anyway," Hornsby said.

In Collinsworth's quest for football knowledge, he has gravitated toward the math people that he was responsible for bringing into the company. He often turns to data scientists George Chahrouri and Eric Eager. But when it comes to advancing the company, Collinsworth's history in football opens doors that otherwise would remain closed to outsiders.

"He has given us a humongous amount of credibility," Eager said. "When we go to places like the NFL combine, he sits in the room with us and everybody stands to attention. He commands that. That adds a ton of value. He's seen a lot of the league. He played his last game when we were three years old. He's been in this thing a long time. Having that know-how is a big deal."

As we walk through the park that separates the hole-in-the-wall restaurant from the PFF office, Collinsworth remembers the first time he became enthralled with football analytics.

On November 16, 2009, the Indianapolis Colts were playing the New England Patriots and naturally, with Peyton Manning and Tom Brady quarterbacking, the contest came down to the final moments. Belichick called for a passing play on fourth down late in the game despite the ball being in New England territory and widely received criticism when the play failed and the Colts won the game.

"I remember doing the broadcast and my initial thought was, 'What the hell is he doing?'" Collinsworth said. "I'm thinking, I know Bill. Bill scored [highly] on his SATs, he's not stupid, he knows the numbers and he knows what Peyton has been doing and he knows if he punts this ball back to him. That was really the first of the eye-openers for me."

Now that data pertaining to coaches' decisions is more widely accepted, it's clear that Belichick's memorable decision, which went badly that night, was following the right process even if it didn't work out.

As PFF makes more discoveries, Cris has taken great joy in the debates that come along with them. He gets a kick out of being presented with a conclusion from the data scientists and then trying to pick it apart and ask questions from every angle. He loves hearing their responses and digging to the bottom of the issue. He likes to push them.

"What I tell our guys all the time is, 'Don't ever think you have the answer either.' For a lot of years the football people thought they knew all the answers and they were wrong," Collinsworth said. "Now if we start thinking we have all the answers, we're going to be as archaic as they are in their thinking. You need to be constantly challenging each other and listening to people challenging what you're saying and fighting and arguing because that's how we got built. Don't ever lose the argument, don't ever get to the point where you say, 'We cracked the code!' No, you didn't. If you cracked the code, you'd be running the New York Giants and digging them out of a hole right now."

Chahrouri says that Collinsworth's curious mind sets the tone for the entire company.

"The guy is always learning," Chahrouri said. "That's one of the coolest things about him as a leader. He's not going to sit there and go, 'I have it all figured out. I should be the chairman of the year in the U.S.' He comes in and says he's trying to learn every day. He goes and tries to talk to the smartest people he can talk to and that sets an example."

Collinsworth has made the debates and discussions a fundamental part of his broadcasting, trying to first-guess on coaching decisions and pointing out some of PFF's more interesting findings, like the idea that coverage better predicts successful defenses than pass rush. At times during an NBC broadcast, it might sound like he's arguing with himself over the analytics, and he likes it that way.

He wants more new ideas. He stops mid-conversation to talk about how the addition of women and people of underrepresented backgrounds to the company in a recent round of hires has given a new voice to the analysis PFF can provide.

"I've learned the significance of a diversified workforce," he said. "Since we brought in women—which we had hardly any of—and we brought in [people] of all kinds and from all kinds of countries, the conversation is just different. It's just different."

But Collinsworth doesn't want to talk about what PFF has meant to the grander scale of the game of football. Asked about being a major influence in football's analytics movement, all Collinsworth will say is, "That's fair." I asked Neil if he views Cris as a football analytics pioneer. He doesn't think of Collinsworth that way. He thinks of him as the person who took his prized possession and cared for it.

"When you sell your company to somebody, you are very cognizant of what you're doing and you're very much watching the whole time, 'Am I doing the right thing? Is he going to do the right thing by it? Is he going to do the right thing by the people that you've known and you love?' If my expectations were high, he's exceeded all of them," Hornsby said.

In the months after my sit-down with Collinsworth, he and Neil would fundamentally drift apart about the direction of the company following the Silver Lake deal. Collinsworth's original concerns about adding an investment group to the mix may not have come to fruition, but there were unforeseeable consequences, particularly the pressure to find new ways to bring in revenue. Cris and Neil differed on how they should increase cash coming into the business, and key PFF employees ended up on different sides of the fence.

Chapter 10

PFF AND *SUNDAY NIGHT FOOTBALL*

YOU MIGHT NOT recognize the name Fred Gaudelli, but you absolutely know his work. In February 2022, the longtime lead NFL TV producer wrapped his 16th season with *Sunday Night Football* by producing his seventh Super Bowl. He completed his 32nd year overall as the man pulling the strings behind the scenes of NFL broadcasts.

One of the keys to Gaudelli's success: the Sports Broadcasting Hall of Famer has always been willing to try something new if he felt that it would improve the experience for the viewer. He was first to implement the yellow first-down line that you see on every single NFL broadcast these days and he gave the green light to the league's first goalpost cameras.

When Cris Collinsworth called him to explain that he'd discovered Pro Football Focus data and was buying the company, Fred's first reaction was, "*What?*" and his second thought was about how it might be useful.

"I wanted to learn more about their grading system and how they were doing it and I think at that point they might have had a couple of teams that paid them a nominal fee every year to look at their roster and evaluate their players," Fred said. "That brought a little bit of legitimacy to me because if teams were going to pay them money...the fact that a general manager or personnel department looked over their material and said that it might be worth having these guys' [data], that was intriguing to me."

In 2016 the broadcast began putting PFF grades on player graphics and then switched to showing rankings to appeal to a wider audience.

"The big step for us at NBC was not putting the 1–100 grades up there, it was ranking the players," Collinsworth said.

Naturally, not everyone was pleased about the grades/rankings being broadcasted. Offensive lineman T.J. Lang was particularly peeved at *Sunday Night Football* using PFF's numbers.

"They don't know anything about identification, what offensive linemen are supposed to do," Lang said in a radio interview. "They've always graded me well, which I don't mind, but I still don't respect it." Lang also noted the use of PFF grades in NBC broadcasts, saying "I think it's absolute garbage, and I think most players do."

"When you start [showing rankings], now you're coming back and now you've got issues with players," Collinsworth said. "Now when I go to a practice and some 300-pound guy starts walking toward me, all I'm thinking is, 'What's his grade? Do we like this guy or do we not like this guy?' Because I've had both approach me."

Collinsworth would agree with the challenge of grasping all things about a player in one grade but would contend that players who share PFF's positive grades on social media don't see it as garbage. Neil Hornsby has signed jerseys in his basement from lineman Evan Mathis and cornerback Chris Harris, whose "secret superstar" talents were highlighted by PFF.

Gaudelli thought the grades gave an interesting snapshot for viewers of the type of performance a player had put together for a given season. After all, he understands that not every viewer knows every team's nose tackle and left guard. He also recognized that context was difficult to achieve on a single graphic. But that part also worked in the broadcast's favor because it became a point of discussion.

"There are times where I'll see a player ranking—like a Devin White, who I think was in the 80s last year among linebackers—basically saying there are 79 better linebackers than Devin White, which is hard to imagine because Devin White has this sterling reputation—but they're grading every aspect of Devin White and, sure, he makes a lot of splash plays and a lot of spectacular plays," Gaudelli said. "But according to PFF he blows a lot of assignments or he freelances a lot, and they grade him down for that. It's a combination of information that at that point no one else had, the ability to bring to light greatness at positions that don't have statistics and maybe have some information that runs counter to a general perception of a player."

"As PFF grew, their grading system and tape review and all that stuff got more precise and it had to pass through more levels. I kept feeling more confident about it all the time," Gaudelli added.

The NFL didn't like the idea of having the grades on TV. For what reason is unclear. Maybe it was similar to what Reed Albergotti reported years earlier about the league and teams not wanting fans possessing All-22 coaches' film. But Gaudelli insisted that the grades made the broadcast better.

"There is no person [Fred] is not prepared to piss off, there's no person he is not prepared to throw under a bus to make that production better," Neil said. "If he thinks that production is better, he will do whatever it takes. That's his genius. An unadulterated focus on making the production the best it can be. He is always, 'This is about the game. It's not about you, it's not about me, it's about the game.'"

What did it mean for the grades to be on *Sunday Night Football*?

"It was utterly huge," Neil said. "It felt like this massive vindication of everything that we'd been doing."

Grades were hardly the only thing that Gaudelli wanted to use. PFF held a treasure trove of numbers that could bring some light to what was happening on the field. He remembered the days when getting a good replay angle of a receiver's foot being out of bounds was a huge challenge. Now Gaudelli was able to give NFL fans the exact time from the snap to the ball being released from Tom Brady's hand. He could look at every single snap between a pass-rusher and a left tackle in their careers and see who was getting the better of the matchup. He wanted any numbers that explained what makes players great or showed players' struggles. They all tell a story for the audience.

"Especially for players who don't have statistics—offensive linemen; other than sacks, defensive linemen—you're able to illustrate why they are great or how they are great in ways that you couldn't do it in the past," Gaudelli said.

But with great statistics comes great responsibility. Gaudelli knows his audience's thoughts and feelings the same way you know your best friend. He hears what they hear. He sees what they see. And he understands that if the stats get too convoluted, viewers are going to be confused as all hell.

"I have a rule: If I can't understand it in 20 seconds, it can't be on television," Gaudelli said. "If I can't explain it or if it's not readily explainable on its own, then we're not going to use it. That's my No. 1 criteria. That's basically all you have between plays. That eliminates a lot of stuff."

While Gaudelli is steering the ship and calling the shots on which stats make the cut, he says none of it would work without Collinsworth having a similarly strong idea of what fans watching the game are looking for and how to explain the numbers without being confusing.

"Cris understands the audience," Gaudelli said. "He understands what the audience needs and when they need it. He's also fearless. But he's not coming with a hot take, he's coming with a well-formed opinion, but he's not afraid to tell people what he really thinks and that happens a lot less often than it should in my business. He can flip the switch between analytics and storytelling and straight-up analysis, so he's able to weave all of that through a broadcast. There's not many other people who can really do that."

Before putting all these things on TV, the NBC crew does its weekly meetings with each coaching staff. There, Collinsworth is aided massively by having the data by his side.

"He may go all-in on a guy that no one else is talking about because he has nine games' worth of data on this guy and then when he talks to the coach, he can say, 'Hey, [Player X] at nose tackle, he's having a hell of a season, isn't he?' First, the coach won't believe that Cris even knows about his nose tackle and then he'll really give Cris some good information because he knows Cris has done his homework," Gaudelli said.

Gaudelli describes Cris as having a "blissful" way about him, where he doesn't outwardly appear to get stressed by the sheer amount of work on his plate or by all the people who want something from him at all times.

Here's an example: at the NFL combine, Collinsworth was standing inside a hotel lobby chatting with another PFFer and a writer from Kansas City when several people walked over to him and said, "Are you Cris Collinsworth?"

This is a bit unusual at the combine, considering most people in Indianapolis for that week are connected in some way to the NFL—meaning they wouldn't have to ask whether he was Cris Collinsworth. But it turned out these folks were there for the annual meeting of the American Association of Swine Veterinarians. Collinsworth signed a napkin and stood in a circle asking the vets where they were from and what they did. At one point, one of the vets apologized for taking up so much of his time. He thanked them for stopping over, turned around, and went back to talking with his colleagues about why Brett Favre was a winner.

"He's got the right mind-set," Gaudelli said. "He's got a mind-set that I wish I could have."

I ask Gaudelli why he thinks Collinsworth wants to run PFF with such a hands-on approach and why he wants to go out of his way to hunt for every detail when he's reached a point in his broadcast career where he could ease off the gas. Not to say that he could mail it in, but...

"But he could..." Gaudelli says.

Yeah, he could. Why doesn't he?

"I think he saw the potential and I think he thought that his name would provide some legitimacy within the league," Gaudelli said. "I think he saw the future in a big way. That analytics was going to become a bigger and bigger influencer in decision-making.... I don't know if he saw a legacy project, but it's going to be a legacy project for him."

PFF can only be part of his legacy if people recognize it.

The Ringer's Kevin Clark brought up a good point on this. He said that if there were a museum dedicated entirely to Cris Collinsworth, his work with PFF wouldn't get its own wing—it would probably get a display. His playing and broadcast careers would get wings.

But the massive leap in influence over the football world PFF took under Collinsworth's watch would be enough to fill the whole museum. And it should be recognized that Fred Gaudelli's insistence that PFF's data be part of the *Sunday Night Football* broadcast played a big role in that.

Chapter 11

THE DRAFT

Few people benefited more from Collinsworth's purchase of PFF than Mike Renner. The decision to track college games has helped Renner to become one of the most respected NFL draft analysts in the media.

He also represents a bridge between the Originals and the Next Wave of PFF employees. Renner was at the center of Neil Hornsby's battle with PFF shifting from a start-up to a mid-sized company that couldn't be operated autocratically anymore.

Mike was born with a particular strand of DNA that made him love the NFL draft. When he was 10 years old, he started asking for draft guides for his birthday, which happens to fall around the same time as the draft every year. His goal was to figure out who the Green Bay Packers, his favorite team, were going to pick. Mike got his whole family in on it. They began having draft contests where everyone in his family would make their picks and whoever got the most Packers selections correct was the winner. He's still proud of nailing the Najeh Davenport pick in the fourth round of the 2002 draft. By his teenage years, Mike was buying every draft guide he could find. On the *Madden* video game, he didn't care about playing the actual games. He only wanted to fast-forward to the offseason so he could draft players and build teams.

Mike Renner has established himself as a foremost expert on the NFL draft by combining scouting with PFF data.

When it comes to finding a career, sometimes the answers are right there in front of you, but you can't see them because of everyone else's expectations. That was the case with Renner. He went to Notre Dame to be a doctor because his father and older brother were doctors. He failed out of organic chemistry as a freshman, so that path was DOA. He tried accounting, hoping that he could at least have job opportunities out of a career he didn't care about doing. But by his senior year, his GPA was so low that getting a job in the field was going to be really difficult. He didn't want to go back for his MBA, because that meant more school and more school sounded like torture. Similarly to Nathan Jahnke, he took a shot at becoming an actuary and passed two exams. At least he'd have a career and make money, but it was far from his passion.

During the spring semester of his senior year, Mike saw that Pro Football Focus was hiring "analysts," which really meant player participation trackers and potentially graders.

Here's where Renner was different from his predecessors: he had to fight through a big crowd to get an opportunity at PFF. It wasn't like the old days of Steve Palazzolo or Rick Drummond emailing to get their hands on data. There were 300 people who attempted to track the practice games. Renner came out in the top 150 during the first run-through. And then he discovered the place on PFF's site where he could cross-check the next round of tracking. Mike was among the most accurate in his "class" of trackers and was hired. He didn't tell anyone until years later that he'd had the answers to the test.

Mike was tracking games part time and waiting tables in Champaign, Illinois, when he decided to bail on the actuary thing and give PFF everything he could. Though it was a far cry from being the next Mel Kiper Jr., he knew this was a chance to get paid doing the only thing he'd ever cared about: football.

He started piling on as many games as he could—though it turned out that without the answers, Mike wasn't a savant like Nathan Jahnke when it came to player participation. So Neil asked if he wanted to go through Ben Stockwell's process of learning how to grade the games. That's when it clicked. The once-unmotivated 2.9 GPA student who skipped classes at Notre Dame because he couldn't bear the thought of one more accounting spreadsheet suddenly kicked into high gear. Mike bought football books and asked more questions than Bobby Slowik, the former Washington coach, could handle.

"I wanted to know everything I could about the game where I could defend any opinion that I had to experts," Renner said. "I wanted to be an expert."

Renner became one of the best graders on the PFF staff and when Collinsworth bought the company, he was the first out-of-towner not named Neil Hornsby to move to Cincinnati. That's where he met up with former NFL quarterback Zac Robinson, who was on staff as well, and started deep-diving on every detail of QB play.

"Picking those guys' brains was so invaluable because as much as you can read stuff out of a book and watch the game, having someone who has lived in it and been in it actually explain it to you, you're not going to be able to replicate that," Renner said. "That was how I went about it."

But once Mike arrived in Cincinnati in 2014, he realized that the company was in a state of flux. Did he come all the way here just to do the same grading that he could have done at his parents' house back home? Even in the aftermath of Collinsworth's purchase, there was a brewing divide over the team data element of the company and the media side. Renner told a colleague soon after he moved that Neil Hornsby would someday need to move aside if they were ever going to make progress on the media side because Neil saw PFF as a data company first, with the media stuff being ancillary.

He may have been happy to have the chance to grade games and write articles—including a piece in 2017 about how the Patriots struggled to cover formations that put three or four receivers on one side of the field—but he wasn't thrilled with the lack of commitment to spreading PFF's innovation to NFL fans. Imagine how pumped teenage Mike Renner would have been to have all the ideas that PFF was capable of talking about…and yet he felt they weren't doing enough to share them with NFL fans. Renner was doing YouTube videos in a closet, and they were getting as many hits as your parents' Facebook posts.

One of the things that frustrated Renner was that Collinsworth had pushed for PFF to track college data and they were barely using it publicly to give themselves an edge over other media companies. The 2018 PFF "draft guide" was just a bunch of stats in PDF form.

"I'm thinking, 'I'm going to leave if we're not serious about this becoming a thing,'" Renner said.

He went to Neil and asked to be in charge of draft coverage.

"We were missing the boat on this whole industry that's become massive," Renner said.

"I was so upset about not having a draft product because the biggest single market differentiator for us is collecting all that data for 130 college teams," Renner added. "Literally no one has ever collected it. If I had that as a kid, I would have been ecstatic. That's all I ever wanted as a kid was to have that sort of data that didn't exist. You'd be like, why is this guy with 1,200 receiving yards ranked below this guy who had 500 yards last year? That never made sense to me as a kid. Now I can explain to you why, there's a lot of data points where we can explain to you why."

Neil agreed to put Renner in charge of the draft. The timing was perfect to start making a real impact on how the NFL viewed the draft. Renner's data-driven analysis was paired with being able to use PFF Ultimate to gain perspective on potential draft picks that no other draft analysts had. PFF was also starting to build a data science team that produced fascinating draft studies. As the math wizards like Eric Eager, Kevin Cole, and Timo Riske dug into topics like positional value, which positions translated quickest to the NFL, and which NFL combine events had the most correlation to NFL success, Renner was able to combine the data with his eye, which had been trained by grading games and the guidance of Bobby Slowik and Zac Robinson.

"There really was no [draft analytics] back then," Renner said. "Not that I know of. Nothing that was on our radar. The initial use of PFF, the whole thing around what we sold to teams was purely about game planning. There was no advanced college scouting aspect to it."

While Renner believes that player evaluation is the slowest aspect of the NFL to come over to the data side, the changes in teams' approach started to become more visible. PFF's ideas about positional value weren't completely original, but they came with more data science behind them and came at the right time as the NFL was moving forward with numbers. In 2018, only three teams drafted running backs in the first round, a sea change from the league's past valuing of RBs. Only four were taken in the first between 2019 and 2021, with the highest selection being 24th overall. The analytically driven Cleveland Browns drafted much younger players than anyone else in the NFL because they found better odds that 20- or 21-year-olds would succeed than 24-year-old prospects.

PFF ramped up its studies in the subsequent years as tracking data came available. Renner paired these ideas to give insight into draft strategies that were unique in a crowded space. For example, PFF intern Tej Seth discovered that the tracking stat "Completion Percentage Over Expected" had a correlation with quarterback success in the NFL. The CPOE data showed that none of the quarterbacks in the 2022 draft were particularly outstanding in comparison to their peers of the recent past.

In a video released by the New York Jets, the team talked about using its own CPOE model to influence drafting quarterback Zach Wilson. In the clip, Jets director of analytics Brian Shields says, "He completed about 12.5 percent of his passes over what would be expected.... He had the best metric among Lawrence, Fields, and Lance on tight-window throws."

Renner ranked the QBs, including Malik Willis, whom some projected as high as the No. 2 overall pick, lower than the consensus.

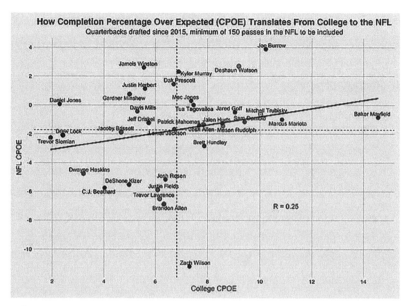

Mike Renner uses data to guide his draft analysis, such as this chart created by PFF intern Tej Seth that analyzes QB completion percentage over expectation.

"A lot of the talk surrounding this year's quarterback class has been focused on the top-five quarterback prospects (Malik Willis, Kenny Pickett, Desmond Ridder, Sam Howell, and Matt Corral), and how they aren't quite as capable as previous quarterback draft classes," Seth wrote. "This is backed up by each draft class' CPOE in their last season in college before entering the NFL draft."

On draft night, the league took only one quarterback in the first round and let Willis slip to the third.

The data insights haven't always led Renner's takes to match up with NFL teams'. He ranked edge rusher Trevon Walker as the 12th-best prospect, which was quite a bit lower than he was taken (No. 1 overall). His take was justified by an analysis done by data scientist Timo Riske, who analyzed whether performance in the NFL combine or production in college was more telling toward future success and found that, after adjusting for draft position, college production was a better indicator than athleticism and that it was possible teams overvalued their own ability to develop pure athletes, particularly at the top of the draft.

Riske wrote:

> On the one hand, this could be driven by league-wide over-confidence in the ability to develop the potential into on-field success. On the other hand, this could be driven by the problem that measuring athletic traits via combine testing comes with uncertainty to begin with, and the real difference between a 90th-percentile athlete and a 75th-percentile might be smaller than we think.
>
> We also found that the better alternative at the top of the draft is to forego [sic] a bit of freakish athleticism if you can select a prospect who was much more productive in college. In this year's draft, this would mean choosing Aidan Hutchinson and Kayvon Thibodeaux over Travon Walker at the top of the draft. The time to shoot for upside through athletic traits might start with Day 2 of the draft.

Renner had his share of hits and misses like everybody else. In 2020, for example, he identified Boise State edge rusher Curtis Weaver as a potential analytics gem and ranked him as the 26th-best player in the draft. But Weaver went in the fifth round and two years into his career, he had already played for multiple teams and had appeared in just one NFL game. That same year, Renner ranked quarterback Tua Tagovialoa as his No. 2 player and Justin Herbert as the 30th-best prospect in the draft. Herbert became an instant superstar. So did Justin Jefferson, whom PFF had ranked as the 32nd-best player.

However, Renner was able to spot some fool's gold, including first-round bust K'Lavon Chaisson, whom the Jaguars took in the first round but Renner had as the 46th-best prospect. Same for linebacker Kenneth Murray, a first-round pick who didn't work out in his first few seasons. PFF's big board scored him 62nd. He nailed three other first-round busts in tackle Isaiah Wilson, guard Austin Jackson, and cornerback Damon Arnette, grading them as borderline third-rounders.

With each hit or miss comes a new study of what went right or wrong. Every one of them is progress toward his analysis—and NFL teams—nailing the fickle draft. Renner says he has seen his big boards coming closer and closer to the NFL's draft decisions.

"We're getting our first data for what translates from college to the pros and continuing to hone in better and get actual better information and feedback than what we've ever had in the past," he said. "We're just going to keep iterating, keep getting better and keep finding the areas that players need to succeed, where players need to be good at the collegiate level to succeed at the NFL level."

As of 2022, the NFL's hit rate on first-round picks was just under a coin flip. By the second round, it was one in four players making it to become quality starters. Renner thinks there is a lot of room to grow using data with his own analysis and inside NFL walls.

"I think the next frontier is tracking data and utilizing that because that takes your eyes and bias out of it to a degree," Renner said. "No one is ever going to get to a perfect hit rate.... You're never going to eliminate situations like that, but I do think your first/second round hit rate there are enough good players that you can get to an 80 to 90 percent hit rate of guys who are competent starters on your football team. That's very realistic."

It's rare that teams go into detail about how they are trying to close the gap using analytics, but former Minnesota Vikings general manager Rick Spielman talked about his process on a podcast with Steve Palazzolo. Spielman detailed that his analytics staff kept a database of all the players they scouted dating back 15 years, which they would use to compare to every new draft class.

Here's what he said, via an article from football writer Paul Hodowanic:

> To give you an example, a left tackle, we had maybe really liked a guy. But…his arm measurement was less than 33 inches long and he ran a 5.25 or slower 40. Well, [our] analytics [department] said there have been seven guys with those measurements that came in and were drafted in the first three rounds and none of them ended up being starters or being significant players in the league. That would throw a red flag up for me and for us as we went through the decision process.
>
> We used a lot of that as tiebreakers, I guess. Some guys, we had a dump box at the bottom of each category. So if there was something that was a major concern for us, then we'd pull them out of the cleaner guys and put them in a box to say if he's still there in the later rounds then maybe we take a swing at him. You're not even adding in the character side of it, the security background checks that you did. What we found was that if they had a medical red alert and a character alert, and a lot of that was discussed when we were in the group setting, if they got two of those red flags, we would take them off our draft board. Because analytics came and did a study over the last 15 years [on] how we graded them medically, and again that's a subjective grade because everybody's doctor grades differently and character, [but] if we put them as a red flag character guy, that combination [with a medical red flag], there was a zero percent chance of that guy ever playing to his grade, where we had him on our draft board. That held up over the last 15 years.

The analytics department was also key in helping identify late-round and undrafted fliers. Spielman said the team averaged about 110 players on its draft board that were "Viking fits," meaning they matched the schematic, character, and film requirements the team needed to use a draft pick on. But they had about 700 more prospects on their "back board," which was filled with mostly undrafted players. Spielman said the analytics team was able to eliminate about 650 of those players each year based on different historical thresholds that indicated that the player would have a hard time even making a practice squad. With the remaining players, the department was able to identify a few prospects per position group that could have a chance of making it.

"It really helped us to bring those guys to the forefront. So we knew of guys that could potentially have a chance," he said.

Star receiver Adam Thielen, quality punt returner Marcus Sherels, and longtime fullback CJ Ham were all players whom the analytics staff "pinged" as having NFL potential.

Toward the end of Spielman's run, he said the front office almost got to the point of "cloning" players, meaning it had such a deep repository of data that the team could find nearly exact comparisons with current and old draft prospects based on measurables, production, and character.

What Spielman's comments tell you is that teams are pouring resources into the draft more than ever. It also says that someone like Renner is using a lot of the same tactics to talk about the draft as people inside front offices.

But he came close to not having that opportunity. Renner, who has more than 70,000 Twitter followers and the top-three draft podcast on the iTunes chart during draft season, almost never made it to PFF prominence because he was fired by Neil Hornsby and had to fight to get his job back.

In 2017, Renner got caught in the middle of a miscommunication between managers. Khaled Elsayed had sent directives for everyone to grade five games per week during the summer, but Neil had requested Renner create some separate reports for teams. Assuming Neil's request took precedence, he focused on the reports rather than tracking the games. When Neil confronted him, Renner explained the mistake and said he would get working on the tracking, not understanding that Neil wanted all the games he had missed to be done at once.

Renner asked to work from home on a Friday with plans to take off halfway through the day for a Las Vegas weekend. Neil called Renner right before he was boarding and asked why he hadn't finished tracking the games.

"[Neil] said, 'I need you back at the office, if you're not back at the office by the end of the day,' he's cursing and saying, 'You're motherfucking fired,'" Renner said. "I'm like, 'I'm not going to be back in the office by the end of the day.' He just hangs up. I call back, no answer. I'm like, I just got fired."

When PFF was first getting built, Neil's ability to push everyone to the max was arguably the No. 1 reason why the company became a success. He demanded hours that no sane person would put in and kept an even crazier work schedule himself. But with Collinsworth in command, the company settled in Cincinnati, and non-Originals like Renner expecting a certain decorum to be held, there was a natural conflict. Growing up as a company meant no longer being able to haul off and fire people based on a whim. Neil found that out with the Renner situation.

On the plane, Mike composed an email to the human resources department, explaining that he'd been canned over a management miscommunication and made note of Neil's swearing tirade. By the end of the day Monday, Renner had his job back.

"It's like he treats PFF like everything is still his," Renner said. "If you are doing something and not following orders, you are basically personally attacking him by not doing so, that's how he's approached pretty much everything in the company. One of the bigger stories the last five years was that he wanted control of everything, as soon as he had a thought of, 'Do this,' you had to do it or else you were personally affronting Neil."

"Putting the fear of god into people and having them work ungodly hours is kind of how PFF got built, but once we got bigger and had a bigger vision to what the company should be, his day-to-day micromanagement was a detriment," Renner said.

Neil regrets what happened with Mike. Too often, he says, he would become fixated on work ethic and took it personally if he felt someone was slacking. It's part of the reason he was able to initially weed out people in order to form the Originals who built the company, but his over-the-top standard couldn't apply to everything and everyone all the time as they grew.

"I was wrong, 100 percent; there was no reason for me to do that," Neil said. "Mike is one of the smartest football people I know. His football knowledge is excellent...he made the pitch to become our draft analyst and he's the No. 1 draft analyst anywhere, and that's not me blowing smoke up his ass.

"I learned from that incident that the company was growing up, and I couldn't handle things the same way that I had going forward."

In 2022, Renner announced a new solo podcast called *Talkin' Ball*. His fourth episode featured Chargers head coach Brandon Staley. It seems the newfound structure in place that allowed Renner to get his job back played greatly in the company's favor.

Chapter 12

COACH'S CORNER

Pro Football Focus changed the way Paul Alexander coached offensive linemen.

"I used to be caught up more in the X's and O's and the schemes and the adjustments…but it's more now about figuring out how to block the guy you have to go against and all the different techniques," Alexander said over the phone. "There weren't enough hours in the week trying to figure out all the pressures that a particular player had that year. You'd have to watch all the tape. Now you can pull up all those pressures in moments. It completely changes the productivity of the working hours of the NFL coach."

Alexander played football at Division III SUNY Cortland in the late '70s and early '80s. He had a great offensive line coach who inspired him to go into coaching. The Western New York native first went to Penn State as a graduate assistant under Joe Paterno and then spent two more years in the same position for Bo Schembechler at Michigan. In 1987 he got his first college job as an offensive line coach at Central Michigan. It was there he realized that he was good at it. He also discovered what type of coach he was going to be.

Alexander explained that there are different types of coaches. Some are what he called "relaters"—the Tony Dungys and Pete

Carrolls, who connect with their players on a deeper level and focus on culture. There are "searchers," like Bill Walsh—those who are on a never-ending quest to find new football innovation. Lombardi, he said, was a technician who spent a lifetime perfecting every step of the Packers Sweep. Tom Landry and Bill Belichick, in his opinion, were "analysts." They were analytical in nature. That's how Alexander sees himself. And that is why PFF's data appealed to him.

After cutting his teeth in the Mid-American Conference, Alexander coached New York Jets tight ends for two years and then moved back to coaching O-line in 1994 with the Cincinnati Bengals. It was there he would spend the next 24 seasons—15 of them as O-line coach/assistant head coach. In the early 2010s he noticed that journalists were starting to quote PFF grades in articles. He was intrigued. While some coaches insisted that people outside of their building couldn't grade their players, Alexander thought it could help him figure out which games to watch on film. Before each game, he would look at how other offensive linemen performed against the next upcoming pass-rusher and then point his superstar left tackle Andrew Whitworth in the direction of fellow tackles who both succeeded and failed.

"I'd say, 'Whit, watch these games, this guy blocked him good,'" Alexander said. "Then I'd pull up which games the guys didn't block 'em good and I'd say, 'OK, and watch these games here because he wasn't blocked good,' and I used it as a way to filter out study. That's how I originally used it."

As Alexander used the grades more often, he came across some plays where he didn't agree with PFF's takeaway. So he sent Neil Hornsby an email.

The response he got from Neil was, "The only thing I care about is getting it right and making it better."

Alexander loved that. The reality about offensive line play is that absolutely nobody walking planet Earth understands offensive line play except offensive linemen and offensive line coaches. But in order to provide the most accurate data, PFF needed to fully grasp which types of blocks should get positive, negative, and neutral grades. Paul was happy to help PFF get it right. He and Neil talked regularly and sometimes debated how to grade certain types of blocks, always with the intention of doing it in the best way possible. Alexander essentially became PFF's offensive line mentor.

"[Neil] understood as the company's influence grew the responsibility he carried with the grades," Alexander said.

The grades became a deeper part of his coaching process. At the bye week every year, he would look at every negatively graded PFF play from each of his linemen and then chart the reasons that something went wrong. He would look for patterns and develop points of emphasis to coach his players on during the second half of the season. He would do the same thing at the end of the year, giving players feedback on what they needed to emphasize for the following season.

Once PFF unleashed Ultimate on the NFL world, Alexander was a kid in a candy store. Suddenly he could click around and find all sorts of different types of blocks, situations, and matchups.

"I would break down matchups of two different players and pull the video up and study them and break them down and come up with game plans of how to block them," Alexander said. "In the later years of my coaching and with the consulting that I do, it completely redefined my role as a coach."

When he works with college players and uses the same tactic of studying their negatively graded plays, the legendary O-line coach will sometimes get pushback from the player about PFF's grades. So he'll pull them up and ask the player which plays they disagreed with.

"If there's 30 plays on there, probably 28 of them myself and the player are going to agree that, yeah, that's about right," he said. "I don't think the acceptance rate of current coaches and their ability to whiz around Ultimate is where it will be in the future. Believe me, once you go through that and you see that—it was enlightening to me."

Alexander believes that PFF's grading has completely changed the way we view offensive line play because it gives the world statistics to use in the same way that receivers have catch totals and quarterbacks have yards, touchdowns, QB rating, etc.

"It's going to put two of my players, I believe, in the Pro Football Hall of Fame," Alexander said.

He's referring to Willie Anderson and Andrew Whitworth. For Whitworth, PFF's numbers have been influential long enough for the football world to accept his greatness. His stint with the Los Angeles Rams, which included a Super Bowl victory to cap the 2021 season, gives him a very good shot at the Hall despite having only four Pro Bowls and two All-Pros. According to Pro Football Reference's Hall of Fame monitor, there are no offensive tackles with fewer than five Pro Bowls to make the Hall, yet the Pro Bowl metric for linemen is now considered vastly outdated. Instead, voters can look at the fact he is the highest-graded lineman of the PFF era.

Anderson is a different story. He also has four Pro Bowls but his final season in the NFL was the first year in which PFF began grading linemen. In February 2021, Alexander asked Neil if PFF would go back and grade Anderson to provide some type of context to his overlooked greatness.

While they couldn't get enough game tape to look at all Anderson's seasons, the graders did find Alexander's intuition about Anderson was correct when looking at the 2006 season.

They discovered Anderson only allowed 11 pressures that year, which would have been the fourth-best season in the PFF era.

"For years, offensive linemen have made the Pro Bowl and Hall of Fame based on popularity and other reputations," Alexander told The Athletic. "But analytics like Pro Football Focus have now changed all that. Offensive linemen now have stats. And there's a way to fairly and objectively set the discourse.... When Pro Football Focus objectively grades Willie, he will have ammunition."

In December 2021, Anderson made his first appearance on the Hall of Fame finalist ballot. While he didn't make it with the 2022 class, Alexander believes that he will be in soon enough.

Alexander uses the examples of Whitworth and Anderson to teach his younger players. His message: if you want to get recognition, you have to grade well by PFF. Contracts, Pro Bowls, and Hall of Fame bids are all being influenced by the PFF data.

But how does one go about grading well?

"The key to having a good grade is being consistent," Alexander said. "It's not how many pancakes you get, it's how many blocks you miss. Until a player accepts that, they can't grade well. And if they can't grade well, they don't get paid."

Even in retirement, Alexander does offensive line consulting and enjoys helping young linemen. He has a Patreon in which he posts offensive line content. He still "lives" in PFF Ultimate, watching tape and looking over O-line data. He tweets about offensive line play. In fact, in his Twitter bio, he points out that his offensive linemen had the highest combined pass blocking grade during his time in Cincinnati. And he notes his pride in coaching 16 Pro Bowl linemen. If he hadn't had to catch a flight, Alexander would have spent another hour coaching me on O-line play.

So before he had to run, I asked him about Neil. What's his legacy to people inside the NFL?

"He changed the game, he really did," Alexander said. "He changed the ability to set a value on players based on objective data. The whole ability to study not only just players, but schemes and situations and things at a level never done before."

"In my mind, I believe this: I think the work of PFF and the work he did is worthy of the Pro Football Hall of Fame."

Paul Alexander is far from the only coach in the NFL whose career was impacted by PFF.

Long before Zac Robinson watched from the sidelines as quarterback Matthew Stafford led a Super Bowl–winning drive on the back of an iconic no-look pass, he was doing grading for PFF. Before that, he was a backup quarterback in the NFL hoping for a chance to show the league he could play.

Robinson was a three-year starting quarterback at Oklahoma State, where he compiled 66 touchdowns and led two nine-win seasons for the Cowboys. Despite a down senior season statistically, he was drafted by the New England Patriots in the seventh round of the 2010 draft. He was cut out of camp but found a new home in Seattle for several months. When he was let go by the Seahawks, the Lions picked him up and then in 2011 he found a spot on the Cincinnati Bengals' active roster as a backup.

While he didn't get into a regular season game, Robinson threw an incalculable number of practice passes, which eventually wore on his arm. He needed Tommy John surgery. He wanted to continue the fight for a long NFL career but reality set in: it was over.

Robinson wasn't the type to put football aside and go into finance or sell insurance. He got started training young quarterbacks in the Dallas area and started thinking about what might be next. Like many of the PFF Originals, Robinson was intrigued by the Pro Football Focus website and figured they had access to film if they were grading players.

"I wrote them an email introducing myself, not really thinking much of it, just 'Hey, I'd like to see what this is all about.' And then ended up hearing almost right away from Neil," Robinson said over the phone from Los Angeles.

Robinson talked with Bobby Slowik about his experience working with PFF and was intrigued. Two months after his feeler email, Robinson flew to Cincinnati. Steve Palazzolo took him through the quarterback and offensive line grading processes, and they were interested in Robinson helping with defensive coverage analysis. Coverages are one of the most challenging things in football to decipher on tape and Robinson had the experience of seeing them on the field and studying them in NFL meeting rooms. Nobody else at PFF before that could say the same.

Robinson connected with Neil on a different level right from the start.

"Nobody was going to outwork Neil," Robinson said. "He was like a quarterback in terms of his process. He'd work out in the morning and he's so regimented, he's up there early and staying late, it was like a franchise quarterback with his work ethic. It pushed everybody else to want to stay on his level...you knew right away that, man, this guy has a great football mind. He always wanted to talk quarterbacks, and we'd fire back and forth and I'd love hearing his perspective on a guy and it might make me look different at a draft prospect coming out or something."

As Collinsworth was taking over the company in 2014, Robinson agreed to come aboard on a part-time basis while still training QBs in Dallas. By the next year, he went full time, cross-checking all the quarterback and receiver grades and working on studies for teams. He was able to give feedback to Ben Stockwell on the grading system and improve areas that only a quarterback's eyes could see.

"We continued to sharpen it and say, 'This shouldn't be on the QB because this angle of the route, him coming out of this thing threw off why the ball location wasn't where it was,'" Robinson said. "I think knowing how routes were run by receivers and those types of things helped out because it's easy to see a quarterback overthrow a ball and everybody points out, 'What in the world was that?' Well, what is the reason for that? We ended up sharpening it up pretty good and getting guys looking at how routes are run and how the receivers impact QB play so much."

It wasn't exactly where he'd pictured himself being in his late twenties, but Robinson was getting something out of PFF beyond access to a ton of NFL tape: a direction. Many former players struggle with finding their way in the real world after the NFL dream dies. Robinson was instantly given a way to stay in the game and a purpose to work toward building PFF and growing his own understanding of the game.

"There are so many of my buddies that—it takes a while," Robinson said. "It takes a couple years. There's very few guys that I know that have it set up.... Of course, you have things that you want to do in the back of your mind but until that actually hits, you don't really know.... I was working with these quarterbacks in Dallas and some of these college guys preparing them for the draft and pairing it with PFF and being able to have unlimited access to film and hearing different perspectives of the game, it was huge, man. It was a great thing to have. I will always be forever grateful to Neil and those guys for getting me on board and staying in the game right after I got done playing."

Robinson's tape-studying skills may have been more advanced than his PFF colleagues, but as he was watching every throw of every NFL quarterback, things started to click in his mind. He started teaching young QBs tendencies that he noticed from watching the likes of Drew Brees, Aaron Rodgers, and Russell Wilson. He looked for commonalities in their fundamentals and how they made the same things work but in different ways.

Robinson spent several seasons behind the scenes at PFF before landing an interview with Sean McVay only weeks after the Rams had reached the 2019 Super Bowl. He used all of the information at his fingertips to land a position on the Rams' staff as assistant quarterbacks coach.

"The amount of stuff that helped me from PFF was huge," Robinson said. "Preparing for that interview, I was able to take a deep-dive into the 2018 season for the Rams. I knew a lot about their offense. I'd watched every single pass snap and had studied their film a bunch and really was able to take a deep-dive in terms of Jared Goff's quarterback fundamentals and their scheme, and all of that helped in terms of the preparation for the interview. I ended up getting the job the next day.

"All the experience with PFF and being able to reference things that Sean would bring up in the interview with other teams around the league. 'Have you seen Drew Brees take three steps on his quick game from the gun?' Being able to have that knowledge from watching and seeing all the snaps around the league pass-wise that season was huge. It all came together, but no doubt the help from PFF and having that access to watching every single snap was instrumental in helping me get the job."

As a member of the Rams' staff (Robinson was bumped up to QBs coach and pass game coordinator in 2022), he's still using the PFF data in many of the same ways as when he was cross-checking games.

"We use PFF Ultimate every single day. Every single coach on our staff," Robinson said. "The amount of resources and the database that those guys have built for coaches and scouts and personnel people to be able to go to their website and load up video and cut-ups, the access that we have to be able to see things around the league or study ourselves and different teams, has completely changed the game."

Los Angeles Rams quarterback coach Zac Robinson
helped PFF shape its grading system before becoming
an NFL assistant.

"More people should know about Neil Hornsby for what he's
brought with PFF and what it's done for the NFL," Robinson said.

On the matter of Stafford's no-look pass, Robinson said he isn't
sure that even the PFF grading scale he helped upgrade could
quantify the magnitude of that throw.

"I think that's off the scale, the play that he made in that
moment," he said. "What an unbelievable play."

Robinson has a ring because of that play—and, in part, because
he joined on with PFF right after his playing career ended.

Chapter 13

THE BALLAD OF
AUSTIN GAYLE

A T 16 YEARS OLD, Austin Gayle left home when his dad tried to set him on fire.

By his mid-twenties, he was bringing direction to Pro Football Focus' growing content side like it had never seen before, co-hosting the third-ranked NFL draft podcast on the iTunes charts with Mike Renner and producing a podcast special with the No. 2 overall pick, Aidan Hutchinson.

When he was born, you would have given Gayle about a zero percent chance of thriving. He was the product of two broken people. His father was the son of a meth dealer for the famed biker gang the Hells Angels and his mother was put up for adoption at birth and suffered physical and sexual abuse growing up. Austin's father learned to grow marijuana at nine years old and became an alcoholic by the time he could drive. His mom stole cars.

Gayle's parents divorced when he was three. His dad was addicted to hard drugs and worked as a mechanic to make ends meet, but he couldn't provide for the kids. Gayle and his sister lived with their mother, who battled drug addiction as well. She had a new boyfriend with a job, but that relationship didn't last

Austin Gayle overcame a difficult upbringing to become one of PFF's most valuable employees.

long and his mother turned back to a hobby of hers from before the kids were born: grand theft auto. You own it, she could steal it. Had carjacking been a laudable profession, she would have been giving lectures on it around the world. Instead, she was dragging the kids from hotel to hotel, stealing cars and then leaving them when she felt the heat. Stealing a U-Haul truck was a bridge too far. She was arrested with the truck. Gayle and his sister were put in a holding area for kids whose parents had been jailed.

Gayle's father picked them up at the holding area and vowed to get sober to raise them. Austin was seven years old, and his sister was nine. They were about to add a stepbrother to the mix. His dad was having a baby with his 22-year-old girlfriend, who had dealt with trauma of her own growing up. She wasn't ready for motherhood, especially not three kids at once. She turned abusive, leaving Gayle and his sister with black eyes while his father worked 12-hour shifts. Gayle remembers burying his sister's report card in the backyard so his stepmom wouldn't find out that her grades were bad. He remembers missing school because it was too obvious that he'd been beaten. He remembers his sister getting it worse.

When Gayle was around 14 years old, his stepbrother Vincent was diagnosed with cancer that would eventually kill him. They drove 30 minutes each way every day to the hospital in San Francisco to be there for chemo, radiation, and the horrors of cancer.

Gayle's sister eventually had enough of the abuse and went to the police. His father took the fall and his sister left for foster care. His stepmom left when Austin was 15 and his dad started drinking and doing hard drugs again.

"Cocaine is a hell of a drug," Gayle said. "You do it for a long time and the lack of sleep creeps in and it will change your fucking life. It will turn your life upside down."

One night, Gayle's dad told him that the house was on fire. After a quick inspection, he tried to convince his father that nothing was wrong and then went to bed. He woke up to his dad lighting his blanket on fire.

That's when he ran away.

He went to stay with a friend named John Marsh. After 10 days straight of staying at his friend's house, John's parents, Tom and Shannon, started asking if everything was OK. For the final two years of high school, Gayle stayed there and had little contact with his parents or stepmother.

"Those two years with them...are the only reason why I ended up getting out of that situation," Gayle said.

At the end of high school, Gayle needed to get out of Northern California. He envisioned himself becoming a teacher and coaching football. Growing up, football gave him a reprieve from his home life. He wanted to give that back. But he also wanted to make it somewhere. Was it really possible for somebody who hadn't played football past high school to end up as a major college or NFL coach? Probably not. So Austin picked another route to be near football: journalism.

When Gayle joined the San Diego State University student newspaper, *The Daily Aztec,* he told them he wanted to cover football. Sorry, pal; that's for juniors and seniors. Instead, he wrote about tennis, water polo, and whatever else came up for his first two years. To scratch the football itch, Gayle started his own website called The Draft Pulse. The more he wrote, the more people asked him to write for them, most of the time for free. He can still rattle off the sites he provided free content for: Football.com, EndZoneSports.com, SB Nation, Gridiron Sports, FanSided. Anything that came with a byline. Gayle remains proud of his first hot take of the Draft Pulse era, which was his projection that Khalil Mack would be better than Jadeveon Clowney.

Gayle kept taking every gig that came available. Sports director at the school newspaper, intern with Fox Sports San Diego, you name it. Oh, and he eventually did get to cover the football team when he was assistant editor at *The Daily Aztec.* That's when he started doing some player tracking for PFF.

When it came time to look for real jobs, he got some good advice at a résumé workshop. He was told to leave San Diego if he ever wanted to make it. The weather is too good and the sports aren't relevant. Everybody wants to be there, but there's nothing to cover. Gayle went to work firing out résumés all over the country, 129 in total. He got three responses—one from a paper in Baltimore looking for high school coverage; another from Pratt,

Kansas; another from Lincoln, Nebraska, to cover Big Ten wrestling. Come on down, Lincoln. But as he was mentally preparing for the idea of moving to Nebraska, PFF offered him a full-time position doing customer service.

It wasn't exactly journalism, but it was football. He packed up and moved to Cincinnati nine days after graduating.

When Gayle first arrived in Cincinnati, he quickly developed a reputation for himself as a go-getter. Aside from his job answering customer email questions—boasting a response time of 44 minutes—he would do absolutely anything else that needed to be done, whether he knew how to do it or not.

He picked up side writing gigs, covering a girls' lacrosse championship for the *Cincinnati Enquirer.* He googled lacrosse rules in the car before walking in. He reported on the local ECHL team for $50 an article and covered some Reds games for Fox Sports Ohio. For a paper called *City Beat,* Austin went to a dozen local brunch spots and ranked them. Despite his freelance work for the Cincinnati outlets, PFF wasn't letting him write about football. He won employee of the year in his first year but still couldn't land a spot on PFF.com. So much for the old days of Khaled Elsayed letting anybody write who wanted to write.

Not long after that, in 2017, Neil Hornsby wanted to talk to Gayle about writing, but not in the way he'd hoped. Neil wanted him to quit writing for other companies. Though he was only making in the $30,000-per-year range, Neil cut him off from all the freelance work but still wouldn't allow him to write for the PFF site. Gayle couldn't wrap his head around why Neil was making him choose or why he couldn't get a chance to prove his football writing skill despite his chops being good enough for the top newspaper in town. Gayle also points out that there is nothing in the employee handbook that forbids freelance work for non-competing companies. After all, girls' lacrosse and brunch spots weren't exactly encroaching on PFF territory. But Neil clarified that there was a clause in his offer letter about outside work.

Gayle chose to stay with PFF. He couldn't risk trying to make a living on freelancing.

"I was really frustrated," Gayle said. "I told Neil that if he's not going to let me write, at least let me do things in other places. I need to do more."

Neil told me he didn't fully understand Gayle's desire to be a journalist at the time. He saw Gayle as having rare leadership qualities and wanted to steer him toward the path of becoming one of PFF's future leaders and away from writing.

"I've learned that you can't push people the way you think they should go when it's not what they really want," Neil said.

Still, Neil said yes to Gayle taking any work around the PFF shop he could find. Someone wanted off an editing shift on Sundays. Gayle stepped in. They needed graphics done. Austin stepped in. Marketing? SEO? Video? Gayle was there.

"It was fucking hard to stick to PFF," Gayle said. "The only reason I stayed was because they kept letting me pick shit up."

While Gayle was grinding to move up the ladder, his step-brother was dying. For 10 years he battled cancer before passing away in December 2018.

"You look at the situation he was in, man, can you imagine?" Gayle said of his brother. "It really does put a perspective of the opportunity you have with life…. He was a very big inspiration, he was a very important person in my life."

From his start in 2017 until 2019, Sam Monson oversaw content. Nobody in the company disputes that Monson is a marvelous media personality, great writer, and ace podcast host, but managing is a totally different animal and it wasn't for him. The content side of the company was in relative disorder.

Collinsworth wanted a change. Neil says he wanted to promote Gayle to lead that part of the business but was cognizant of his age and felt that he might be best partnered with someone. After George Chahrouri initially said that he preferred to remain in his research and development position, Neil persuaded him to take on the job and work hand-in-hand with Austin.

"I said: about fucking time," Gayle said.

Chahrouri tried to choke back his emotions talking about Gayle's growth within PFF, in part because he feels like Gayle probably should have waved the middle finger at PFF and left, but instead he gutted it out.

"It makes me sad and mad at the same time," Chahrouri, who is general manager of content, said. "This is one of the reasons I respect him so much, because I like to think I would have been this strong, but the stuff that he went through while working at PFF and got basically zero support from anyone at PFF while living in Cincinnati as a new employee, he didn't know anybody. And he stuck it out."

Chahrouri quickly realized that Gayle was more than a go-getter; he had a vision for what the media side could become.

"I'll never forget, I was in a meeting...for an app concept or something, and it was a cacophony of terrible ideas and he spoke up.... He was a customer service rep. And he raised his hand and he said, 'You know, we make X percent of our money between July and October and it's because of fantasy football. If this app isn't about fantasy football and betting, it's a complete loss.' I was like, 'Oh, there's someone here who isn't full of themselves and looks at data and has a coherent thought.' From that moment on my opinion of him changed considerably and I paid more attention to what he had to say, and then when Cris asked me about switching over to the consumer side and running that, the first thought that I immediately had was, what an opportunity to leverage to give Austin an opportunity to be great."

Chahrouri and Gayle went to work organizing the writers.

"The first thing I did was double his salary and say, 'You're in charge of getting our content schedule in the right place; let's figure this out and figure out what talent are writing,'" Chahrouri said. "When I tell you there was no pitch process, there was no organization schedule, there was no alignment between editorial and writers, there was no weekly conversation between editorial and writers or leadership and talent. That was honestly, and it sounds mundane, but that kind of process and willingness to work hard enough to put it in place is what helped us get off the ground."

Gayle's idea was that PFF should write what people wanted to read—and with a less adversarial tone. That may sound obvious, but for many years the Originals were fighting an uphill battle trying to get anyone to pay attention to their work. Chahrouri felt that they lost sight of the fact that they had already won over football fans and now needed to change the way they presented themselves.

"This is really apparent if you study the growth of the company. It's like, the mentality that you have that gets you from 0 to 1 isn't the one that gets you to the next step," Chahrouri said. "We had to look at our brand and the way that we talk to people on social media and say, 'What do football fans want to hear about?' And we realized that we were still talking and tweeting and posting as if we were this huge underdog that needed to be super edgy to get anyone to listen to us."

Page views from 2019 to 2021 jumped by 86 percent.

"That's a byproduct of putting people in charge that really give a fuck, that really care," Gayle said.

Gayle thrived in his new role. Aside from taking charge of the organization and directing the vision for the media side, he flexed the muscles he first started working out for *The Daily Aztec* and Football.com back in the day. His podcast with Mike Renner,

PFF Tailgate, peaked on the iTunes chart in the top 20 football podcasts during draft season as the two traveled around the country to podcast about major college games. He also produced an epic four-part series on Aidan Hutchinson. He worked closely with the No. 2 overall pick in the 2022 NFL draft and director of communications David Sulfaro to book dozens of interviews, from Jim Harbaugh to ESPN's Adam Schefter to NFL Network's Bucky Brooks, to produce a complete profile.

Gayle wanted to show that access journalism could be worthwhile to PFF despite some of the challenges that come along with trying to turn a profit with interviews that take commitment from the listener to consume—and that social media aggregators will simply repurpose if there's anything juicy. So Gayle paid for much of the project out of his own pocket, footing the bill for a private plane to transport the Hutchinson family from their home in Michigan to Cincinnati. They were trying to recreate something with a couple people that ESPN would do with an entire crew of professionals.

"It was my bet," Gayle said of his investment in the *Hutch* project. "This is on me. It's a big swing of the bat. We had pressure to make it worth our while."

"It was super meaningful," he added. "If an opportunity presents itself that's unique and rare, regardless of how difficult it could be to do it, you have to fucking try it…it was a lot of learn-as-you-go. It was learning how to direct, produce, script with people that were underpaid and underappreciated and did not sign up for this…and we did it. We fuckin' did it. It was cool to be in the David and Goliath situation when we were competing with companies that have more money and more interest in supporting projects like this."

Naturally, work like that garners attention from those media companies interested in supporting projects like *Hutch*. A few weeks after the draft, former ESPN personality and founder of The Ringer Bill Simmons emailed Gayle a job offer. A few weeks later, he left PFF.

For timeline purposes, it needs to be said that a lot happened in a short period of time between Chahrouri and Gayle taking over the consumer side of PFF and Gayle leaving for The Ringer, and those blanks will be filled in throughout the coming chapters. At the time Gayle was producing *Hutch* and partially funding the project on his own dime, Neil was already away from the company and said he wouldn't have allowed that to happen. Neil had been gone from PFF for several months at the time Gayle made his announcement about his new position and was crushed to find out he was leaving.

"How the fuck did we lose Austin?" he said.

Part of losing Austin was the simple fact that he wanted to write and talk about football, and The Ringer gave him a bigger platform to do so. But that wasn't the whole story. Gayle was also caught in the middle of a battle over the future of the company that left him frustrated and willing to try something else.

At the back patio table where we sat, Neil fiddled with his phone to show me something. It was a video he'd made announcing Gayle would be inducted into the PFF Hall of Fame, breaking one of the rules that an employee had to be there for at least 10 years.

Neil starts out the video by saying, "When I first got to know Austin, I'd go for walks with him and try to get to know him a little bit better and he told me that he was looking for three things in his career: he wanted to do football journalism, number one. Number two, he wanted to make enough money to sustain his family, and number three, he wanted to be part of a winning team. I thought to myself, 'We can do all of those things.'"

Neil shakes his head, still seeming to be in disbelief that Austin had taken another job. Neil wasn't used to people at PFF just...

leaving. It hit him as a sign that things at the top of PFF were already going in the downward direction he had spent months worrying about.

"Austin and I will be friends forever. I've always looked at him as a little bit of a son in a strange sort of way. I always wanted the best for him," Neil said.

Chapter 14

DATA SCIENCE

Five years before George Chahrouri became Cris Collinsworth's right-hand man and arguably the most influential person inside PFF not named Collinsworth, he was teaching math in Compton, California, at Verbum Dei High School.

Chahrouri got a math degree from Loyola Marymount University because he felt like math would be applicable in any type of field, but he felt particularly drawn to education. Out of college, he landed in the Teach For America program. He spent two years in Bridgeport, Connecticut, before moving back to his home state of California. Throughout his upbringing, Chahrouri had been an obsessive fantasy football player and a heated competitor. He played in his first for-money fantasy league at age 11 and lost $200 when he was coaxed into a terrible trade.

"If you asked my mom to tell you about me as a kid, you'd get a lot of funny comments, but one of the things that you'd get is that I was the worst loser on planet Earth," Chahrouri said. "I wouldn't cheat, but if I lost a game, my god. Tears. It was bad. This didn't matter if it was Monopoly, UNO, basketball championship, fantasy matchup. Ever since I was a little kid, nothing has been more painful for me than losing."

Once a teacher, George Chahrouri became a right-hand man to
Cris Collinsworth.

He was a savvy kid too. Chahrouri spent a lot of time growing
up around his local municipal golf course, to the point where the
pros got to know him. They would give Chahrouri the promo-
tional golf clubs that were sent to them by club makers and he
would sell them on eBay and then split the money. That helped
pay for the clubs he broke on the course.

During his teaching career, Chahrouri stoked his competitive
side by trying to gain any edges he could in fantasy football and
gambling on the NFL, while also using sports as a driver to teach
math lessons to kids. He started getting interested in building
mathematical models and went in search of football data that he

could work with. That's where he discovered PFF's fountain of data. Though he was irritated at the lack of a robust fantasy section (which he would eventually play a central role in improving), PFF had officially caught his attention. During his fourth year as a teacher, Chahrouri saw a tweet from Cris Collinsworth that the company was hiring. Interested in finding out how they got all the data, he applied and landed a spot collecting data.

"I was like, 'They've gotta have people there doing math, right?'" Chahrouri said. "They had no one there doing math."

When Chahrouri joined, PFF's analysts were using the grading system and doing studies that were moving the needle, but they simply were not trained in advanced mathematical techniques and model-building in the same way Chahrouri was. Collinsworth began to recognize the value of advanced math and saw the possibility of pushing PFF to another level with it.

In 2017 Collinsworth started building a data science team that included Eric Eager, PhD, who took notice of models that Chahrouri was building and wanted him to be a bigger part of the group. They bonded over betting models at first. Together they would start taking hold of influence within PFF that nobody outside of the Originals ever had before.

Up until that point, PFF had gotten its edge by having more data. Nobody else could tell you how many snaps a cornerback took in the slot, for example. Nobody could tell you how he did in coverage in detail. That was all gained by the player participation trackers and graders. But how much did that same slot corner matter to winning? How valuable was he to a defense? These are the types of questions that PFF couldn't answer anywhere near as accurately as Collinsworth wanted. So PFF hired Eager and Chahrouri full time.

"As data scientists we were thinking about how we could help teams win more games, and that's a hard thing to figure out," Chahrouri said. "A lot of it was, how can we sharpen our own intelligence? We can work on our own ability to predict things and learn about different players and different strategies and all those things. There also wasn't a ton of structure around math."

Chahrouri's skill for creating visualizations gave him an opportunity that would eventually lead to him becoming an Emmy winner and one of Collinsworth's most trusted employees.

When PFF first worked out a deal to provide data to *Sunday Night Football*, Neil was putting together packets of statistics for Fred Gaudelli to use on the broadcast as he pleased. Neil would wake up before dawn each Monday and start furiously gathering everything PFF had on the upcoming week's game. It was a long process, in part because the data had to make sense and tell the right story. He would often hunt for numbers to back up an idea, only to find that the stats said something different than he expected. On a good Monday, about half his potential notes for Gaudelli got in the packet, and if he was five minutes late, his phone would start ringing with Gaudelli wondering when he was getting the info.

Part two of the process was Gaudelli going over every note with a fine-tooth comb and quizzing Neil on their relevance and accuracy. One time, Gaudelli was told that PFF had credited a player with fewer QB pressures than another outlet. So they went to the tape to look at all the pressures play by play.

Neil loved that about Gaudelli. The level of detail was exciting. But it was also time consuming. When Neil took over the CEO role, Collinsworth told him that someone else had to be assigned to *Sunday Night Football*. Enter: Chahrouri.

Chahrouri and Eager were brought to Cincinnati to give a presentation to Gaudelli. They showed Gaudelli a model to estimate football players' Wins Above Replacement in the same way that exists for baseball. The duo also developed a fourth-down decision-making application. Gaudelli wanted more where that came from.

Gaudelli was skeptical of someone new taking Neil's spot, but Chahrouri quickly earned his trust. Chahrouri could put the packets together quicker and make the visualizations look much better. Instead of 25 sheets, Chahrouri could throw together 50 sheets in the same time span.

Chahrouri ended up in the NBC truck, offering an analytic view on the game for Al Michaels and Collinsworth. During games, PFF analysts furiously grade each play. That information ends up in Chahrouri's hands, and he decides what goes into the broadcasters' headsets.

"Sometimes you may not pick up on a guard on an unbelievable night or a safety other than an interception and a couple of tackles or a tight end blocking his ass off," Gaudelli said. "If you're the second tight end, you're probably not getting a lot of tackles, you're not catching many passes, but you might be having a dominant night and the key to this team being able to run outside. For me, it's like, OK, this might help me tell a more complete and accurate story of the game with them grading it, but I can't be talking to these graders during the game. I'm focused on what Al and Cris are talking about. I'm focused on what's on the screen. Cris thought it would help him."

Gaudelli liked that Chahrouri could bring predictive analysis to game situations. He built models that could compare the chance that a pass had to be completed, which added context to a ridiculous pass or catch. His work could cross-check and provide specifics to the broadcast as well. Say, for example, that a coach told the SNF crew their team was expecting to see extra linebackers used against their rushing attack. Fred would ask Chahrouri how many times opponents played extra linebackers against that team earlier in the season. When the matchup of said linebackers versus the team's offensive line happened, Chahrouri could point out who was winning.

"He was there as…almost a combination of a statistician and editorial person that might help me tell a more complete story about the game that we're watching," Gaudelli said.

Chahrouri joked that he was mistakenly put on the Emmy list and that his mom is the only one who cares about the awards, but Gaudelli doesn't see it that way. He views Chahrouri as having added something fresh to a production team that was already producing the most popular sports show in the United States.

"He's a guy who really understands high-level mathematics and predictability and things of that nature, but he is also a huge football fan and loves football and he's able to marry those two things," Gaudelli said. "He has a really infectious personality, he's really enthusiastic. You can't give him too much work. The more you load on him the better he gets.

"He's a tremendous asset."

Along the way, Cris and Chahrouri talked a lot about the company, where it was headed, and how it could best grow. In the same way that Chahrouri was once able to spot opportunities to sell golf pros' demo clubs on eBay, he also saw holes in the way PFF's media side was being handled. Tables on the website didn't look quite right on an iPhone. The social media presence wasn't competitive with other large media companies. The fantasy football and gambling products weren't strong enough. There wasn't a clear process for how articles got written and posted.

"There were some gigantic problems that content couldn't fix just by writing a better headline," Chahrouri said.

Subscription models for content were just starting to become more prevalent in sports media with the launch of The Athletic and ESPN+. Collinsworth and Chahrouri talked about how there is only so much data NFL teams will buy, but the number of people who might purchase a PFF yearly subscription is endless. There had to be a plan to grab more fans' attention. PFF could no longer be just for the football nuts—the Rick Drummonds and Steve Palazzolos of the world—if it was going to grow. It needed to be for a regular fantasy football player who loves their hometown team. How could they engage the normal *Sunday Night Football* watcher?

The investors at Silver Lake agreed that the consumer side had the growth potential they were looking for.

At first Chahrouri was hesitant about taking over the consumer department. He was here to help with the math part, not run a media company. He eventually agreed in part because it gave him an opportunity to promote Austin Gayle and start rolling out new ideas.

Chahrouri got to work solving the aforementioned problems. But that came with some complications. Neil Hornsby believed at its core PFF was a business-to-business company, not a media/consumer giant.

Chahrouri taking the reins meant a sea change. The Originals had almost unequivocally been in the leadership positions before Chahrouri took over. His plan was to change the tone from that of the plucky start-up with hot data takes to more of a mainstream media organization, with some unique stats included.

The plan, which Chahrouri was tasked with executing, was to invest in products that NFL fans can buy—to release a PFF app and go all-in on fantasy football and gambling tools. Chahrouri wanted to get the social media team to be more positive and set their goals by positive engagement on social media posts rather than just raw numbers. After the Silver Lake investment, they started building a news team with salary cap expert Brad Spielberger; traditional reporter Doug Kyed, who worked for NESN in Boston; and Ari Meirov, who built a massive Twitter following tracking NFL news.

"You can't do things the same way forever and expect your advantage that you may have gained by doing it that way at the start to continue," Chahrouri said.

But things did not go smoothly. Chahrouri took over the consumer side in November 2020 and by the fall of 2021, Neil was seeing some red flags in the numbers. They were spending the new money from Silver Lake but not seeing the growth in revenue to keep up. Neil wanted to move Chahrouri back to the research and development wing, but the two butted heads over that idea, which felt like a demotion to Chahrouri. They went on a walk, as Neil often does to have serious conversations with employees, and got into an argument over Chahrouri's future. Neil was displeased by Chahrouri's reaction to the proposed change. People within the company began to feel uneasy about the tension between Chahrouri and Neil. The next step in Neil's mind was to let Chahrouri go. But Collinsworth did not want to demote Chahrouri, nor did he side with Neil about limiting Chahrouri's power or giving more resources to the data side.

Multiple PFFers told me that Neil's concerns went beyond dollars and cents. Numerous people inside the building noted that Neil was worried about Chahrouri's lack of management experience, even prior to their blowup. One particular incident caused friction between them: PFF was sued by a former employee who was working under Chahrouri—a social media person who claimed mistreatment. Multiple sources said that PFF paid out $20,000. A source said it was the only time PFF was ever sued. You have probably learned enough about Neil at this point to understand how much that would bother him.

"There were obviously some disagreements over how things should have been done [with changes in the direction of the company]. I think at some point if you're not having those disagreements, then you're not moving forward," Chahrouri said. "I wasn't going to be a part of PFF if they didn't want to be great and didn't want to take every opportunity.... That's why a lot of people work at PFF. We don't pay the highest salaries, we don't give people stock options. The reason people come to PFF is for a chance to be great."

Throughout the fall of 2021 and into early 2022, Collinsworth looked for a solution to the tension with Neil, Chahrouri, and disagreements over the company's direction as a whole. At one point, Collinsworth appointed Neil vice chairman, but they were simply not on the same page. Collinsworth lost a lot of sleep over it.

"For PFF, it's a small company that hasn't had a lot of change and change is hard, man," Chahrouri said. "It can become emotional very, very quickly and it became very emotional for Neil very, very quickly."

Neil ended up taking a sabbatical starting on December 31, 2021, with plans not to return. He announced his retirement late in the summer of 2022.

Some inside PFF wanted to be all-in on the new direction. Potential seemed high in the spring of 2022 for some people who had been grinding on the content side for a long time to get their breakthrough. Young analysts Anthony Treash, Ben Linsey, and fantasy football guru Ian Hartitz were building followings and looking to get more creative with their consumer products.

"We're only scratching the surface," Mike Renner said in May 2022.

But the excitement was met with a splash of cold water when Gayle left. A few months later, the numbers hadn't recovered and there was a nervous feeling that people who had been hired to build the content side would end up losing their jobs. Collinsworth considered another restructure that would build a consumer team to guide the content.

The Originals have been shaken up by the change. They had never known a PFF without Neil steering the ship.

"The saddest part of all of this is that it feels like the business is being pulled apart," Mike Parker said. "I've always cheered for the consumer guys because we're all the same team, but it's starting to feel like it's not the same team. They have their objective, and we do what we do on [the team business side], and we don't really care about each other anymore. It's faceless and anonymous and that's been hard."

The massive investment from Silver Lake and rocky times on the consumer side bring with them some questions about the future of the business side. Bryan Hall wonders if not succeeding with media products as much as they are projecting will cut into what PFF has accomplished with the teams.

"I worry about Silver Lake coming in and suddenly adding $1 to $2 million in additional profit this year won't be sexy, it won't be exciting," Hall said. "Any other company would look at that and be like, it's another great year…these are things that are huge for those people and the rest of us, but don't mean anything to a Silver Lake.

"If it starts to eat into the business-to-business side of what we do, are we going to be the vendor that teams love to work with, which has also helped us keep competitors at bay?"

Neil was also a commanding presence at the top of PFF. Hall said that he set a certain standard—sometimes absurdly high— that he's worried might fade now that Neil isn't in charge.

"That's one of the things that's going to be missed with Neil. I see a little bit of softness already," Hall said. "We have some of these weekly meetings where they are not quite as tight or prompt as they used to be because Neil isn't there. There's other things that as we've gotten bigger as a company from an HR standpoint where we had to be more professional and, 'Hey, we're a real company now and we can't work people 80–90 hours a week and pay them pennies.' My work-life balance is a lot better now, and I'm glad, but you do wonder what that means long-term for our culture and our ethos."

As things grew more challenging, more people reported issues with how they were treated. Those still with PFF say that Chahrouri was critical of their work to the point of them losing confidence, and things got more uncomfortable when he didn't have Austin Gayle to play good cop anymore. Others felt directionless by the fall of 2022. It was not a secret to others within the company that the tension also played a role in Gayle's exit. As close as he and Chahrouri had been coming up through the company, they became distant as he advanced, and Gayle's belief that they could accomplish their original lofty goals waned. When The Ringer called, Gayle felt relieved to move on from PFF's anxious environment.

It's hard to imagine the stress Chahrouri was feeling as he took on the uphill battle of building the consumer side without having managed in the business realm before. As this book goes to print, his future within the company is uncertain, and everyone is unsure about what's next for the consumer side. There's still hope they can get things rolling in the right direction, but there's also pressure to find quick solutions with Silver Lake expecting results.

"I hope that it works out," Mike Parker said. "Because [Chahrouri] is smart, he's tireless, and he's focused and has so much energy, he could actually pull it off."

Throughout the tumultuous times, Chahrouri has worked closely with Cris Collinsworth's son Austin, who played football at Notre Dame and earned an MBA from the Mendoza College of Business. Out of college, Austin worked as vice president of digital media at PFF from 2015 to 2017, but that position wasn't a great fit, so he took a job at a credit card service company called Xsolla, where he was director of investment and partnerships before coming back to PFF in 2020 as chief operating officer.

Cris cares deeply about keeping PFF a family business, so when Austin returned as COO, he appeared to be on a path to grow within the company and ultimately take over Neil's spot as CEO when Neil retired. But when there were disagreements over the company's direction, Neil felt like it was three versus one and fretted over Austin's inexperience in a leadership position. When Neil stepped aside, Austin moved into a key decision-making position, which caused some consternation. The Originals never had anyone except Neil and Cris guiding the ship.

"Austin understands business really well and where we're trying to go. He has been really, really important," Chahrouri said.

One PFFer said they hoped there wasn't pushback from the longtime employees against Austin solely based on his being Cris' son.

"Would you rather this be run by the Collinsworths or have the company get bought by a venture capital firm and be gutted?" the person said.

Austin Collinsworth did not respond to multiple requests to be interviewed.

In early December 2022, Neil's fears were realized when PFF fired 16 full-time employees, including reporter Doug Kyed and data scientist Kevin Cole; numerous other contributors; and even its paid interns. Investigative reporter A.J. Perez, who works for the website Front Office Sports, published a report on the job cuts, citing an anonymous PFFer as saying "it was a mixture of nepotism and stupidity."

PFF provided a statement to FOS: "The Silver Lake investment has fueled the company's consumer growth strategy, building off the foundation of our B2B teams business. We are refocusing our resources into building out our consumer sports betting business."

The firings and the report rocked the building. Collinsworth attempted to find the source of the comments to FOS while employees feared for their futures with the company. One person described PFF workers feeling like the "walls are crumbling."

Chapter 15

AN INFLUENTIAL VOICE
RISES AND EXITS

W HILE GEORGE CHAHROURI was moving to the front of the line in PFF's leadership structure, Eric Eager was becoming one of the most influential people behind the scenes in the NFL.

At the NFL combine, Eric sat in a restaurant with an NFL executive from a recent Super Bowl–winning team and talked over suggestions for adding a wide receiver. He explained that tracking data showed that the receiver's speed could translate to the team's system to replace a player whom the club planned on parting ways with later in the offseason.

When the signing was announced weeks later, it hit Eager how far he'd come in such a short period of time. He thought about how he once told his closest friend in college that he wanted to someday pair his love for math and passion for football together in a career, but there were simply no careers in football data. He reflected on his playing career at Minnesota State Moorhead as a blocking tight end and how he always had this feeling that he knew more about football than the coaches—and his senior-year offensive coordinator in particular hadn't liked that very much. He thought about how close he was to leaving the University of

Eric Eager brought data science to PFF to study the game in ways that had never been done before.

Wisconsin-Lacrosse, where he was a math professor, for St. Olaf College and putting his football dream to the side.

Only days after the combine, he found himself at the Sloan Analytics Conference at MIT, listening to Kevin Clark, analytics pioneer Brian Burke, and former NFL player Mitchell Schwartz debate studies that he'd published for Pro Football Focus. It was another how-did-I-get-here moment.

Eager got here the same way everyone else did. He saw on Twitter that PFF was hiring data analysts and applied, and though he wasn't initially that interested in being a data collector, there was a type of moth-to-flame effect between himself and the company. He quickly became one of PFF's top trackers.

"I was collecting all NFC North games, and my Saturdays were two college football games, Sundays were two NFL games, and I'd do half a *Sunday Night Football* game," Eager said. "My weekends were immersed in football."

Not long after he mastered the data collection process, the editor Jeff Dooley, who eventually left for the *Washington Post*, put out a call for anyone who wanted to write articles for the website. Eager pitched 15 story ideas and Dooley let him write the "best value free agent signings" of the 2015 offseason.

"I remember I was going on a trip to Illinois State for a math conference and I was one of the speakers at this conference… and I'm so geeked out about this little football blog publishing my article and that's probably when I knew that I wasn't going to be long for being a professor," Eager said.

St. Olaf College offered Eager a chance to leave Wisconsin-Lacrosse and get paid more, which was attractive because the state of Wisconsin was threatening to cut down on teacher benefits and pay. He decided the timing wasn't right to leave. There was an undeniable pull that there might be something in the future with this football thing. He started asking Nathan Jahnke for more data to work with and began using all his math PhD powers to build models. During a long layover in the Las Vegas airport following a friend's bachelor party, he spent seven hours creating PFF Greenline, a tool programmed to give football gamblers an edge.

When he got back from Vegas, Eager started writing more and more. His picks column in 2016 became one of the most-read articles on the website. It became clear to Neil that Eager had the bones of a true PFFer. Neil called Eager on Skype and asked if he'd move to Cincinnati and do football full time. Eric declined, but he agreed to head up a data science team.

During his first trip to Cincinnati, Eager was reading a book called *The Undoing Project* by Michael Lewis, which is about Israeli psychologists Daniel Kahneman and Amos Tversky, who were good friends and pushed each other to develop theories about why people make decisions and the unconscious factors that play into them. Eager was inspired—not by the idea of coming up with game-changing football theories, but rather by having a partner in football data who could push him.

A month later Eager was holding the weekly PFF analytics meeting and going over work that his team was doing. He was impressed by a presentation that George Chahrouri had done, so after the meeting, Eager reached out to Chahrouri and said, "Can I call you someday?" The more they talked, the more Eager felt that he had found his good friend with mathematical skills who was going to push him. He began to highlight Chahrouri's work to the powers that be and pushed him toward the front of the line of the data science group.

In 2018, Eager and Chahrouri were both in Cincinnati when Neil offered them full-time jobs at PFF. They both eventually accepted and moved to Cincinnati, but upon arrival, the jobs weren't exactly what they expected.

"I think Cris Collinsworth knew that we've gotta get the right people here, but I don't think anybody beneath Cris knew how to use us," Eager said.

"People were immediately upset that PFF hired us for jobs that were paid what we were paid and we didn't have to collect data," Eager added. "It was like, 'Oh, these guys just have cushy jobs, they go on camera all the time, they have a podcast, and they mess around with math,' and there was some resentment there."

In early February 2019, Eager called Chahrouri and asked if they should bail on PFF. Chahrouri talked him out of it, and a few weeks later Eager sat in meetings with all 32 NFL teams at the combine.

What Eric brought to teams were answers.

PFF's strength had always been the ability to collect an ungodly amount of data for teams to use in whatever ways they saw fit. If teams wanted something specific, they could go to PFF and get that information. But the question of how to use the data and how much it all mattered wasn't being answered mathematically. If a team wanted to know how often an opponent played a certain coverage, it could get that information easily. If it wanted to know how many wins or points playing one coverage or another was worth, that wasn't answerable until Eager and Chahrouri joined PFF. Eager developed a Wins Above Replacement system similar to baseball's oft-used metric. That resonated with teams. They may not have all been cutting edge, but they understood the concept of players and plays equating to winning.

As Eager was getting comfortable at PFF, the league dumped a mountain of digital tracking data on teams. In 2018, the NFL launched NextGEN stats, which tracked every player's movement on the field. PFF leadership was concerned that the tracking data was their new competition. Instead, Eager's data science team was able to get to work combining the PFF data with tracking data to make assertions about the game that had never been made before. For example, Eager studied which linebackers were the most likely to chase a quarterback's fake handoff and which were the best at running down handoffs.

"The people with the teams, they don't have the time to do the research that we do," Eager said.

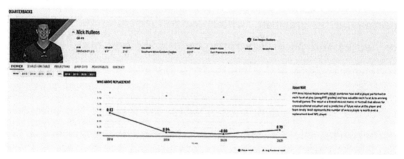

Eric Eager and George Chahrouri developed a Wins Above Replacement system that reflects baseball's most-used advanced stat.

Whether it was Eager's background playing football, his personality, or simply the fact that he could put numbers to things that people had never thought possible, he clicked with a lot of people in the league and became a liaison. Before the Rams played the Bengals in Super Bowl LVI, Eager got a text message from a contact with the Bengals who asked if there was anything they should know about Matthew Stafford.

"He turns into Joe Montana when you blitz him," Eager texted back.

"I'll tell the coaches," the person on the Bengals' side responded.

In the Super Bowl, the Bengals only sent blitzers after Stafford eight times and he roasted them each time, going 8-for-8 with 59 yards and a touchdown. On non-blitzes, he completed just 56 percent of his passes and had a 72.9 passer rating.

Eager isn't allowed to talk about all the things he studies for teams because the clubs agree to a contract that keeps the information private for two years (unless they want to buy more years). After two years, Eager can publish the work publicly. A few examples of studies that have made noise around the NFL:

Eager and Chahrouri looked into whether coverage or pass rush is more important to defensive success. They found that during the PFF era, teams with elite coverage grades (67th percentile or better) and poor pass-rush grades (33rd percentile or worse) won about a game and a half more than teams with great pass rush and poor coverage. There was a much higher correlation between reducing the opponent's expected point totals if the defense's cornerbacks, safeties, and linebackers blanketed receivers than if pass-rushers beat their man. In the following chart by Eager and Chahrouri (via PFF.com), you can see the offense's performance more directly correlating with coverage than rush.

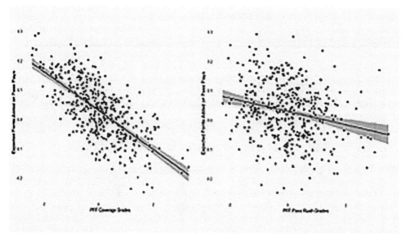

Eric Eager and George Chahrouri made waves in the football community when they found coverage was more valuable than pass rush.

Like many PFF studies, this one didn't end the conversation; it started many more. Part of the analysis found that pass-rushing was more predictable. Year after year, the top defensive linemen in pressure rate continued to pressure the QB, whereas corners could bounce up and down from year to year. There is also the idea of whether quarterbacks are mentally impacted more by defensive linemen getting in their face than they are by corners covering well. Where do "coverage" sacks fit into the mix? What about quicker throws and less time to cover for cornerbacks?

This ties back into an idea Steve Palazzolo posed early in his PFF writing: What is actionable? Should teams only invest in coverage? Not exactly. But this study can be paired with another that found coverage is a weak-link system, meaning that the worst player in the secondary impacts the overall performance of the defense significantly. Resolving major weaknesses, even with average players, in coverage might be as valuable as finding a dominant pass-rusher.

"That the initial conclusions upend some of our preconceived notions but leave a ton of space for new and existing data to be collected, analyzed, and interpreted, makes me excited for what's next," Eager wrote.

Eager investigated how teams perform when their run plays are perfectly blocked and what that reveals about running back talent and how challenging it is to properly block for run plays. He unearthed the fact that only four teams in 2021 had perfectly blocked run plays on more than 40 percent of their runs, and the difference in success between perfectly blocked runs and runs with a blocking error were enormous. Passing, by contrast, survived blocking miscues at a much higher rate—though the downsides to blocking problems while passing are more serious—e.g., a sack, fumble, or interception.

Eager believes this is an explanation for both why coaches love running the ball and why passing has statistically proved to be more efficient. The running plays work with huge success when perfectly blocked, so coaches think if the players simply execute their assignments, they will have a great deal of success. That's true, except that it's hard for everyone to execute assignments over and over. Does that simply mean teams should lean into the passing game more? Probably, but unless teams have elite quarterbacks, it can be difficult to invite more variance by leaning into the passing game.

Here are some notes on a few other studies done by the data science department:

- Eager mined scouting reports from The Athletic's Dane Brugler, looking for words therein that correlated to success or failure. He could then pair those with reports from the past to give a list of comparable players in a scouting context, rather than just looking at sheer numbers for college players.

- PFF discovered that pressure is more of a quarterback stat than an offensive line one, since quarterbacks' reactions to pressure dictate success/failure/sacks more than poor blocking.
- Eager led the building of fourth-down models that use the expected amount of points for a certain down/distance/field position/score to determine whether teams should go for fourth downs or punt or kick a field goal.
- The team sought to find out how much changing offensive systems had an impact in a new coach's first and second seasons. The jump wasn't as big as you might expect.
- The team discovered offensive line coaches have a tangible impact on offensive line performances.
- Eager and Steve Palazzolo worked together on the PFF QB Annual, which included clustering quarterbacks by their playing style, giving insight into which types of quarterbacks were succeeding or having issues.

The struggle Eager faces is that he's a front-facing personality, with his work showing up on PFF.com, the *Forecast* podcast, YouTube, and social media channels. Sometimes he bluntly says publicly that teams are doing things wrong. And he isn't always right. Eager didn't think the Los Angeles Rams would win the Super Bowl after acquiring Stafford, for example.

"It's not easy. If I told you that I had the right answer to this conflict, I'd be lying," Eager said. "I mostly hold back the information I get from teams."

It further makes things tricky that the *Forecast* podcast is rooted in gambling advice. Right before the NFL draft in 2022, Eager got a tip that linebacker Quay Walker was going to be a first-round pick. He bet Walker to be a first-rounder, won on the 22nd overall pick, and discussed it on the show.

Eager has been able to manage the conflicts of interest without major incident, only receiving a message here or there about tweets or comments on the podcast. The Buffalo Bills in particular weren't happy about some comments questioning their quarterback Josh Allen after the 2019 season.

And Eager has been forced to toe the line often. During the season, he's doing a dozen or more radio and major podcast appearances per week as media outlets have also gravitated to his loud voice and unabashed takes. He plays a similar role to Sam Monson, except instead of being the punching bag for talk hosts grilling him, the hosts ask for more of the data-based opinions. Even something as old-timey as talk radio largely changed its approach to analytics and numbers experts.

Eager felt like the Originals were uneasy about his and Chahrouri's growing presence and power. Eager wondered if restructures to the company were aimed at keeping the leadership within those who were there from day one rather than handing the keys to an outsider.

"The people who founded the company really appreciated the work we were doing for the company until it got us power that could change the direction of the company fundamentally," Eager said. "They wanted analytics if it was going to promote their ideas. Anything beyond that or orthogonal to what they envisioned the company being was not acceptable."

"Every single time there was a push, there was a push to diminish, even to the point where promoting me demoted George a little," Eager continued. "If you want to look at it in a sinister way, the moves by the incumbent people have been to use us when they need value and then to demote us when they want their power back."

In his early days with the company, Eager and Neil became close. They worked out in the morning and rode to work together, and Eager would bring his family over to Neil's house. But when Neil attempted to limit Chahrouri's power within the company, Eager believed it would have negative repercussions on his own career, leaving him feeling like Neil had lost sight of an important relationship. Neil rejects the idea that restructures would have held Eager back. He tried repeatedly to tell Eager that he was never trying to hold him back. On the last organizational chart before everything changed with Neil's status, Eager was set to be positioned on the leadership team.

"Cris believes you build a company around your most talented people and you figure it out later," Eager said. "When Neil tried to fire George, who is one of Cris' favorite people in the whole world, he overstepped. That ultimately was his downfall."

Like Austin Gayle, Eager ended up with a front-row seat for the Neil-versus-George standoff over the company's future—and felt manipulated. It ultimately played a role in his leaving.

The new structure of PFF moved Eager from much of his research to a position as essentially Chahrouri's right-hand man on the consumer side. Feeling that their relationship had dissipated, Neil called Eager to hash it out. Neil didn't want to lose a friend in addition to losing his spot in the company he founded, but hard feelings don't fade easily when it comes to careers in a competitive business.

In July 2022, Cris Collinsworth got a call from an NFL GM asking permission to talk to Eager about whether he wanted to join an NFL front office. In the immediate aftermath, he did not leave for a front office job, but he left the door open to that possibility in the future.

Two months later, Eager got an offer to join SumerSports, the project of billionaire hedge fund manager Paul Tudor Jones and his son Jack that aims to create a roster-building tool for NFL teams. The Joneses wooed former Atlanta Falcons GM Thomas

Dimitroff to help them develop an application in which teams can build their rosters through free agency and the draft in a data-driven way.

"It's so similar to what we do with portfolio optimization in our quantitative trading strategies," Paul Tudor Jones told the *Wall Street Journal.*

SumerSports has hired a team of developers to study data and create algorithms that can best predict whether teams are making the right decisions. The model would combine teams' scouting reports with analytics data, which is one of the things Eager studied along the way by looking at which words in college scouting reports correlated to success in the NFL.

If all of this sounds like competition for PFF, well, it is—which is why Eager initially turned down an offer from Dimitroff that would have meant a massive pay increase. He told people around him that he wanted to "see it through" with Chahrouri and PFF.

But that changed in the weeks following the NFL team's interest. Eager lost some of his belief in Chahrouri's leadership—and began to question some of the things he was told during the George–Neil drama. He told Chahrouri about his unhappiness and asked to rework his role with PFF. When the company didn't return quickly with an answer, he decided to take SumerSports' call. He later learned that Chahrouri did not tell Cris Collinsworth about his frustrations and desire to change things. In between, there were debates over Eager's long-term role and even a scuffle over whether he could have Neil's old office. Eager decided it was time for the next chapter and joined SumerSports before the first month of the 2022 NFL season was over. On the day he told everyone within PFF he was leaving, Austin Collinsworth told him about a new plan for his role. But it was too late.

Cris Collinsworth was frustrated by losing the leader of the company's data science team and a popular public face. Eager's exit also represented the first time someone had simply left to join a company that was coming for PFF's territory, which was particularly upsetting to Collinsworth.

Whether it's SumerSports or others, the quick growth of data-driven decisions in the NFL has no doubt sparked companies that will chase opportunities to convince teams their product is better than PFF's.

Chapter 16

THE BIG DATA BOWL

A T THE 2020 NFL COMBINE IN INDIANAPOLIS, a crowd filled with data scientists, NFL executives, and coaches gathered to learn about the best innovations in football analytics.

Michael Lopez beamed as two data wizards, Philipp Singer and Dmitry Gordeev from Austria, blew the socks off the crowd with their presentation on rushing yards. Lopez describes it as the "let's fucking go" moment for the Big Data Bowl, which launched in 2019.

Twenty years (or so) before developing the most prominent analytics competition in American professional sports, Lopez was an undergrad football player at Bates College and a math major. Naturally, when he prepared to do a senior thesis, his subject of choice was football data. However, he found so little to work with in football that he elected to write his paper about baseball instead. Undergrad Michael Lopez would have been over the moon had he known that someday hundreds of influential football people would be in a room captivated by algorithms and tracking data. But that's what Lopez has built from scratch.

In 2018, after years of teaching and occasionally writing about sports analytics, he was named the director of football data and analytics for the National Football League. A major part of Lopez's role is using data to better serve teams and keep improving in areas like health and rules. But the NFL also understood something important that has played out over the last few decades in baseball and basketball: more data means more conversations. The league aimed to push to the front of the line in the ways it could reach its audience.

"The business model is that data can drive interest," Lopez said. "I think in that sense there's quite an obvious link to what PFF has built: where there is newer and better data, you're going to ask and answer more interesting questions about the game you love."

Big Data Bowl is the crown jewel. In 2018, the league provided every team with tracking data, which monitors and records every player's movements in a game. Maybe you have seen on Twitter some plays that are displayed by dots. Those little circles with numbers moving around like the old vibrating football game are churning out mountains of information. Anyone can go to the NFL NextGen website and instantly find out from the tracking data who the fastest players with the football were last year and see route-running patterns from wide receivers drawn out. That's the tip of the iceberg.

While those things are fun to toy around with, they don't answer the questions: How can teams and fans use the new information? What does tracking data tell us?

That's what Big Data Bowl sought to answer.

"This is their new baby; they want to learn about this," Lopez said.

Lopez's idea was to put out a file of tracking data regarding a particular subject and give contestants the task of turning it into something that changes the way the league and fans understand football.

A lofty goal, indeed. And at first Lopez wasn't sure how many people would be interested. In its first year, Big Data Bowl didn't have prize money (it now has a total pool of $100,000), and only a few hours before the first deadline they received just three email submissions. But like one of those reality baking shows in which everybody gets their cakes out of the oven just before the buzzer, the submissions flooded in at the last second, with 75 presentations and 125 total people participating. In the first year, 10 of those 125 data scientists were hired by NFL teams.

"You had club staffers from a variety of disciplines that wanted to know what was the next big thing in football analytics," Lopez said. "What is this Big Data Bowl thing? How can we use it?"

In 2020, winners Philipp Singer and Dmitry Gordeev captured the top prize of $50,000. Something particularly notable about the pair of data scientists: they were not NFL fans before the Big Data Bowl. They run a data science team called The Zoo and decided to try their hand at making discoveries about NFL running games. Specifically, contestants were asked to predict the outcome of running plays based on player tracking data at the time of a handoff.

"Another [data science competition] which we didn't participate in but we kind of followed was predicting quantum bonds between atoms in complicated molecules," Gordeev told Sports Techie.com. "That was probably by far the closest one to the NFL—and I'm not kidding. I'm absolutely serious."

Yes, that's right; they used a model that predicts bonds between atoms and molecules to predict running back success. This is the NFL now.

"It stood out because if you come up with the right question, you can recruit data scientists from all sorts of fields," Lopez said. "They mentioned they used more of an approach that you would more typically associate with biology or physics in terms of how they set it up and the framework and image detection stuff they were using was not how anybody else did it, but was far and away the best way to go about doing it."

The pair wrote this on the website Medium about their conclusions: "We can assess which tactical choices and which individual player performances help the team improve expected running play success, which players contribute more in defending from running plays, which offensive players are better in creating space for running backs and so on."

They were hardly the only group with insightful conclusions. Matt Ploenzke of Harvard discovered that among roughly 40 input variables, a ball carrier's "effective acceleration" was the most important for estimating yards gained on a handoff play.

Kellin Rumsey and Brandon DeFlon from the University of New Mexico determined that Green Bay Packers linebacker Blake Martinez was the best player in the NFL at generating defensive leverage on run plays.

Caio Brighenti of Colgate University investigated each team's control of the field at the moment of the handoff to predict the outcome of rushes and learned that offensive control at the running back's expected point of intersection with the line of scrimmage was the most important predictor of run yardage.

You could fill an entire book looking at all the angles and mathematics on display from only the finalists in only one year and regarding only one subject.

"At some point it will level off, but the steepest part of the uphill graph [for analytics in football] is right now and I'm happy Big Data Bowl has played a big part of it," Lopez said.

Four Big Data Bowls in, the number of participants has more than doubled. Lopez says that more than 20 participants have been hired by NFL teams and another 10 signed on with clubs from other major leagues. For the '22 Big Data Bowl, Lopez worked with PFF's Eric Eager to provide data scientists with additional contextual data to go along with the NextGen tracking numbers. And while some people interviewed said that the NFL isn't happy that an outside company has had so much success in providing data, Lopez says they are using PFF's work to study different elements that may shape future rules changes.

"They have labels that help us save time, and the best analysis of players is going to have the perspectives of merging their information with more performance-based metrics, which you would find in the tracking data," Lopez said. "If you can bind those two together, it's going to be better than each would be alone."

Likewise, Eager uses tracking data to make more discoveries and statements about the NFL. The same day that Lopez talked about the Big Data Bowl, Eager unveiled on Twitter his team's work on which of the NFL's linebackers were most fooled by play-action passes based on how much they moved on a play-fake.

Lopez can speak better than anyone to the usage of analytics and PFF data within the league, and he still can't say for sure which teams are using what numbers. Folks inside the league are so secretive and concerned about espionage that the New York Jets once requested the NFL do a sweep for listening devices before playing the New England Patriots. They certainly aren't willing to open up about data the same way Billy Beane once did in *Moneyball.* However, Lopez does estimate that between 65 and 75 percent of teams are making in-game decisions with direct influence from an analytics person during the game. He notes that if you watch closely during Colts broadcasts, you can see two of their data analysts with headsets on in the booth helping head coach Frank Reich.

"The reality is that [PFF data] saves you a ton of time because you're now able to aggregate a lot of what used to be done using long-winded scouting reports and hours and hours of film. Secondly, you can integrate it with the rest of your analytics processes to get a holistic view of team and player ability," Lopez said. "The hardest thing in football is context. It is every Big Data Bowl; the one thing people have a hard time understanding is the context of what players were asked to do on a play. That is the first thing that coaches think about when they're asked to look at projects—are they able to account for the context of football. If you don't, any finding that might rate players a certain way might be based on the context of what players were asked to do. PFF data is a large subset of the context of what players were asked to do on a play."

In talking about the state of the league and analytics, Lopez brings up this point: while there is some bemoaning of the influence of data in other sports, particularly baseball with its slow pace due to pitching changes and lack of balls hit in play, the NFL's analytics usage has pushed the game in a more entertaining way. Teams are being encouraged to throw the ball downfield more and go for it on fourth downs. If you follow the numbers, drafting big-play machines at receiver and pass-rusher is a must. Offensive creativity and defensive aggressiveness are pluses. Handing off on second-and-10 like many teams did in 2003, not so much.

"One of the really fun parts of football is that most of the suggestions that are data driven make the game better," Lopez said.

Chapter 17

THE ANALYTICS GM

WHEN KWESI ADOFO-MENSAH was introduced as the general manager of the Minnesota Vikings, he was ready for all the questions about his background.

Throughout the interview process, he had been painted as the "analytics" candidate because of his degrees from Princeton and Stanford and his work on Wall Street trading energy commodities before taking a swing at his dream job working in professional sports in 2013. Adofo-Mensah went to the MIT Sloan Sports Analytics Conference looking for any chance to get his foot in the door. There he was introduced to San Francisco director of football administration and analytics Brian Hampton and was eventually hired by the 49ers as a researcher.

Over a period of six years, Adofo-Mensah climbed the ladder to director of football research and development and caught the eye of Cleveland Browns general manager Andrew Berry, who hired him as the vice president of football operations. When Adofo-Mensah was named GM by the Vikings in January 2022, he became the first person with a background purely rooted in analytics to be given the keys to an organization. There were others who had histories outside of being a football scout, coach, or player, but none like him. The 40-year-old's laugh echoed throughout the Vikings'

Minnesota Vikings general manager Kwesi Adofo-Mensah has used PFF data to stand out within NFL front offices.

practice facility when the question about being the "analytics guy" finally came. He made it clear that he wanted no part of that label.

"I remember when John [Lynch] and Kyle [Shanahan] came to San Francisco, we had a meeting where everybody goes around the room and introduces themselves, and I took that opportunity to stand up and say, 'I don't know what analytics is,' and I think I might've laid an expletive in there so I could be extra Football Guy," Adofo-Mensah said. "For me, it's about being thoughtful and intentional."

Cleveland Browns GM Andrew Berry also tried to move away from using the term "analytics" as a way to describe what Adofo-Mensah would be bringing to his new team.

"I think actually a little bit too much is made about the whole analytics stigma, so to speak," Berry said. "I think any high-functioning office, whether it's in the NFL or across other sports, looks to bring different perspectives to the table with decision-making. And using a variety of sources of information, weighing them accurately, allows the decision-maker in any space—whether it's on roster decisions or game-day decisions or medical/performance decisions, contract-management decisions, you name it—allows you to really make the best choice for the organization."

Twenty years after Michael Lewis wrote *Moneyball*, the story of Oakland A's general manager Billy Beane and his unique approach to using statistics that changed the way the sports world viewed applying data to sports, it would be unfathomable for a baseball or basketball general manager to downplay his or her background in numbers. In those sports, anyone without a degree in data science or economics would have to explain to the world how they planned to lean into widely accepted analytical concepts. The last thing you would want to be labeled in Major League Baseball or in the National Basketball Association is "old school."

In the football realm, Adofo-Mensah still felt it was important to explain to everyone that he's just a very educated Football Guy. He talked about learning to write scouting reports when he was in Cleveland. He explained the influence legendary 49ers head coach Bill Walsh's coaching philosophies had on him. He said it was cool to work with Tom Rathman, an ex-fullback who would rank among the all-time most Footbally Football Guys ever. Adofo-Mensah also tried to make it known that scouting was very important to him, as were opinions of players. Again, these things would not be questioned in the NBA or MLB.

Adofo-Mensah's hire and introductory press conference acted as the perfect snapshot to explain where analytics fit into the landscape in the NFL in 2022. The lack of consternation surrounding his hire in mainstream NFL media signified how far football has come in the previous decade when it comes to the acceptance of analytics. But there is still a strong urge to hold on to the idea that the Football Guys know best. The Vikings have only a few employees dedicated to analytics and data, while some baseball teams have dozens. Data is winning, but it hasn't completely won over the NFL yet.

When Adofo-Mensah was climbing the ladder, he knew that he had to find ways to use data to connect to the Football Guys. He turned to PFF.

"The one superpower that I do have is that I'm one of the most curious people you'll ever meet, so if you give me information, I can go use numbers because numbers is my love language, that's how I teach myself things," Adofo-Mensah said over the phone. "Using PFF to teach myself things that, frankly, I didn't know. I knew a fan level, but I had to sit in a room with Vic Fangio and Ed Donatell and Kyle Shanahan and Mike Shanahan and John Lynch and try and understand and keep up with them. How I did that was, I'd take ideas that they would teach and I'd go to the numbers and communicate that way. In doing that, I'd find something that maybe they didn't know or communicate it to them and show them how it works in my language. That's how I built a relationship with those guys. That's ultimately PFF."

Adofo-Mensah used the example of trying to understand the impact of play-action (plays that are designed to look like runs but end up being passes) the same way an offensive coordinator would and then being able to add something to the conversation.

"PFF really allows somebody to go deep and study that for themselves," Adofo-Mensah said. "Now, a play-caller knows exactly why [it works], because you've put people in run-pass conflict and all that stuff, but being able to go through and say, hey first-and-10, second-and-6, the different coverages you get in that situation and is that why? It allowed me to not just do that 'what' but go dig on the 'why' and learn what some of these coordinators who have been play-calling for 20 years know for sure. It allowed me to derive it for myself in a language that I understand."

Around 2015, Adofo-Mensah came across a way that he could bring something fresh to the table that coaches and management would value: PFF's college football data—the same data Cris Collinsworth had pushed his team to collect when he took over the company in 2014.

"You're trying to build college models and you start building combine models and you can only get to a certain point and you're like, 'OK, this is good, but I want to help more,'" Adofo-Mensah said. "So you go looking for sources."

While many around the NFL were hesitant about using outsiders' grades for players, the new Vikings GM dug deep into PFF's grading data to look for numbers that correlate higher with success.

"It always fascinated me that people looked down on the plus-minus model, but I'd go in our coaches' offices and they have a book full of plus-minuses," Adofo-Mensah said. "Well, it seems like they're doing the same thing our coaches do…. They don't exactly know what the person is designed to do, but that's OK as long as that bias is true for everybody they do. As long as they don't know one team better than [another], the randomness and error is going to come out in a wash…. We undertook a lot of validation exercises to see where we thought it was strong, where it could get better, and in the beginning we used what we thought we could use and as it got better we grew with them."

"I do more with PFF grades than most people do," he added.

Growing with PFF also means that everyone else in the NFL has too. In 2015, Adofo-Mensah was ahead of the curve. Now the analytics arms race is on. Teams are scooping up data scientists and PFF is creating more products for them to use, like their IQ system (which, if you remember, pulls in all the PFF data to predict future outcomes for prospects and current players).

"I meet with [PFF] at every combine and I'll look across the table like, 'I love you guys, but I wish you would stop at some point because that cool idea, now 31 other teams are going to have access to it,'" Adofo-Mensah said.

Adofo-Mensah does warn that data in the wrong hands can be a "weapon of math destruction" wherein people use PFF's statistics to confirm what they already believe rather than aiming to learn from the numbers.

"For the people that generally want to search for truth and objective information and help them learn and gain insight," Adofo-Mensah said. "If there's a football Nobel Peace Prize, they probably deserve it. It's helped a lot of things."

When Adofo-Mensah got hired by the Minnesota Vikings, PFF intern Tej Seth was watching excitedly from afar.

"When Kwesi got hired it was the first time I realized that someone who is like me...if they do well when they are working in football and have a couple breaks fall their way, they can actually become the GM of an NFL team," Seth said. "It's something I wouldn't have even considered until Kwesi got hired, that a person with a data and econ background and someone who isn't considered a typical football guy could work his way up and become the GM of a team."

Seth is only 20 years old, but his story of becoming a PFF intern is the same as those who have been with the company for a decade. He loved baseball cards and fantasy football growing up in Detroit and he had curiosity about the game. When he arrived at the University of Michigan, he went in search of others like him. He discovered the Michigan Football Analytics Society.

"About 10 people would show up at each meeting; we'd meet for like an hour like once a week on Wednesdays and talk about what happened the previous week in football and what's happening going forward and how we can use analytics to analyze these teams and these players and stuff like that," Seth said. "It was really cool to have this group of people that were interested in exactly the same stuff as I was, using football stats to be a better fan."

When the meetings got shut down because of COVID, Seth turned his quarantine boredom toward football. He saw a graph Ben Baldwin of The Athletic had created and wondered how he might go about making something like it for himself. He already understood some of the concepts of gathering and organizing data from the information analysis program in Michigan's School of Information but hadn't learned advanced techniques required to emulate Baldwin's graph. So he decided to go find out how to do it himself.

"It was a lot of googling," he said.

The coding community is continuously growing, and Seth discovered that there was a bevy of public work he could borrow from.

"When you run into a problem while coding, chances are that someone else has had that problem and posted about it," Seth said.

After his freshman year, Seth went in search of internships and was growing frustrated that he hadn't landed any interviews. He noticed on Twitter that he followed someone whose bio read "PFF intern," so he decided to send them a message and see if he could connect with PFF. By that time, he'd learned enough about coding that he was tweeting out charts and getting responses from other football fans. Tej got a response and wrote Eric Eager a note asking about opportunities. Eager was impressed with the coding work he'd tweeted out and hired Seth as his new intern.

Over the following few months, Eager would meet with Seth and the other interns every afternoon and brainstorm ideas. One of the most eye-catching charts Seth built was around the time of the draft, in which he showed that the 2022 quarterback class was underwhelming when it came to completion percentage over expectation. While most of the world's draft analysts were predicting anywhere from three to five quarterbacks being drafted in the first round, only one went off the board before Round 2, validating Seth's findings.

He discovered which quarterbacks bounced back the quickest after throwing interceptions, which landed him an interview in The Athletic to talk about Matthew Stafford's short memory following mistakes. Seth also submitted a paper to the Big Data Bowl looking at "optimal" decisions for punt returners between returning, fair catching, or letting the punt bounce.

"Having the opportunity at PFF to reach so many people with the content stuff that we did with these new metrics or The Athletic or The Ringer using something that I built in one of their pieces was really cool, surreal basically," Seth said.

Seth is a slender guy who didn't grow up with a dad who played or coached football. His grandparents moved to America from India. His grandfather came over to get his master's degree from Wayne State University and then worked for General Motors. His grandmother's family dreamed of living in the United States and settled in Atlanta. Seth's parents were early adopters of online dating, meeting in the early 2000s. His dad works for 3M and his mother is a teacher. Someone with his background—non-white, non-football-playing, non-coaching, not tall, strong, or imposing—wouldn't have often ended up influencing the NFL. Football data opened that door.

Part of PFF's legacy and the result of the analytics boom in the NFL is that people like Seth have a place in football.

"The thing I love about it more than anything else is that I think it's brought...everybody can contribute to football," Cris

Collinsworth said. "You can be male, female, any race, from any country, a mathematician, a baseball player, you can be anything and have an influence in the greatest game of all.... You have all these brilliant minds and they're tinkering with this."

That's why Seth was so happy to see Adofo-Mensah get hired. Adofo-Mensah was not a football player or coach. He is of Ghanaian descent. He found his way to the GM's seat through researching football.

"Having been one of a few in many rooms, you talk about Princeton or Wall Street or an econ student or being in an NFL analytics forum and being the only one and where I'm at now, it's special to think that a person might see me and just on the margin believe one percent more in their dream," Adofo-Mensah said.

The Vikings' GM, however, added that his hire doesn't necessarily mean that the floodgates will open and every NFL team will be hiring the next Adofo-Mensah.

"Somebody with my background, right up until I got the job offer from the Vikings, I wasn't really sure that someone would give me that opportunity, if I'm being frank," Adofo-Mensah said. "Just from some of my previous interviews before and, look, there's some things to overcome perception-wise. I'm happy the Vikings believed in me, but they have to actually listen to you and be open minded and that's a credit to them."

More Seths are coming. Eric has three more interns who are already putting out analytical studies, one of which looked at how quarterbacks performed when defenses covered receivers perfectly.

"I took at Tej Seth…he doesn't look like any of us and in previous eras people might have said, 'This person doesn't belong in football,' and I want to be a reason why this person belongs in football," Eager said. "Women in football is another thing. We just got done hiring our first female data scientist for our company. Analytics can do such a good job of getting people into the game that previously for whatever reason nobody thinks this person belongs in the game. Being able to be a part of that growth is huge."

In the same way that Adofo-Mensah once used PFF college data to separate himself within NFL meeting rooms, Seth says the next generation of Adofo-Mensahs will be using tracking data.

"If a team is out there that has different metrics to evaluate players using NFL tracking data, that will give them a pretty good edge when deciding playing time between two players on their roster or which free agents to sign," Seth said. "But the real value to gain is having that structure in place so when college tracking data becomes readily available, they can take that and apply that to the college game and it will really help them in their draft process getting grades for players on their big board because they've already had that set up and don't have to spend a year or two putting in all these different coding measures in place to evaluate college players."

Seth isn't sure if he will be one of those people putting coding measures in place for NFL tracking data in the future. His fellow intern Zach Drapkin got hired by the Eagles as a quantitative analyst after their stint at PFF was over, but Seth hasn't decided whether becoming the next Adofo-Mensah is his life goal. He went back to school and decided to take another internship in a different field to decide whether he'd like to work in football or another area.

"It was cool to pick up on new techniques, whether they were learning new programming tools, learning different ways to talk about football…it definitely helps me for my future as I look to go into the industry of being a data scientist," Seth said. "I feel like I'm more prepared to do that."

Chapter 18

PFF AND THE AGENT

IN 1996, VINCENT TAYLOR played in the NCAA tournament against all-time great basketball player Tim Duncan. A little more than a decade later, he was roaming around the internet for anything that would help him make his case to the San Francisco 49ers that tight end Delanie Walker was worthy of a raise. Intuitively, Taylor knew that his client was a good special teamer and had potential, but there was nothing in the box score to explain the value of special teams. He came across PFF and reached out to Neil Hornsby.

"I was looking at ways to find out how to negotiate with the 49ers and Delanie primarily played special teams, but he impacted special teams a lot, so I knew there was some value there, so I was just searching the internet and I found Neil," Taylor said over the phone.

Taylor started his career as an agent with Capital Sports and Entertainment, becoming certified by the NFL Players Association in 2005. Two years later he went off on his own, starting Elite Loyalty Sports. He now represents a number of NFL players, including superstar left tackle Trent Williams and 2022 No. 1 overall draft pick Trevon Walker.

But when he met Neil, he wasn't there yet. He was looking for any way possible to get ahead as an independent minority agent.

"All the teams subscribe to it now, but back when I started I think no one did," Taylor said. "The teams do their own independent research, but PFF gives you valid points. It gives you a leg to stand on to support what you're trying to get across."

Taylor used his statistical leg to help land Delanie Walker a three-year, $6 million contract, making him the highest-paid backup in the NFL when the deal was signed.

Taylor urged Neil to come to the NFL combine. When they met in Indianapolis, the agent introduced Neil to an assortment of connected people within the league and NFLPA.

While Taylor was one of the first agents to connect with PFF, he was not the only one. One of the first sources of revenue for Neil's company was creating player reports that agents could use for an additional resource in negotiations. PFF would gather the most favorable data and clips of the player's 20 best plays for a highlight package.

When PFF began grading college games, it added another layer for Taylor. He uses the grades to determine which players he should attempt to recruit at Elite Loyalty Sports.

"When it comes to draft time you have all these different people ranking players—[Todd] McShay and [Mel] Kiper—you don't know what they are basing their information on," Taylor said. "You are in a bad spot if you're basing your information on [draft analysts]. PFF has a system that's consistent with the grading.... You have enough data to know that it's within reason pretty close. If a player is rated high or has a good grade, you have all this data over time that has shown whether this player is good or bad. If you have a player that's rated pretty high, it gives a different respect factor."

That agency wing of PFF has grown through the years. Here's an example of a report that PFF has on its website:

10. RAMSEY'S 4-YEAR CAREER FAR OUTPERFORMS HIS PAY

PFF RANKS SINCE 2016 (REG. SEASON ONLY) IN RELATION TO THE TOP 31-PAID CBs (previous slide) ENTERING 2020

STAT	RAMSEY'S #s	RANK AMONG TOP 31
APY $	$5.8M	31ST / 31
PFF OVR GRADE	88.8	5TH / 31
PFF COVERAGE GRADE	90.3	5TH / 31
PFF RUN DEFENSE GRADE	83.5	5TH / 31
TOTAL SNAPS	3,678	2ND / 31
TACKLES	231	3RD / 31
INCOMPLETIONS FORCED	52	8TH / 31
PASSER RATING ALLOWED	76.1	7TH / 31
WINS ABOVE REPLACEMENT	1.92	4TH / 31

PFF WAR, OR WINS ABOVE REPLACEMENT, IS A METRIC USED TO ASSIGN A PLAYER'S PRODUCTION TO A "WINS" VALUE FOR HIS TEAM USING THE RELATIVE IMPORTANCE OF EACH FACET OF PLAY. BY THIS METRIC, RAMSEY HAS BEEN THE 4TH MOST VALUABLE CB IN THE NFL SINCE 2016.

An example of PFF's pitch to agents that uses advanced metrics to help in the company's negotiations.

"The research arm of many agencies is now us," PFF analyst Brad Spielberger said.

While Taylor and early-adopting agents may have gotten help from PFF in the early days, the role PFF numbers are playing in negotiations is increasing as more decision-makers with experience in analytics take over front offices.

"As guys in front offices get younger, it brings more validity to PFF's grading system," said Jason Fitzgerald of OverTheCap.com. "Younger guys come in and they give it merit versus the older guys who might say they don't care about the grades because 'they aren't in my locker room or know what the play calls are.' These GMs now who are in their thirties, they are going to be much more open to those kinds of things."

Taylor is elated to see that the company he used to get ahead early in his career became influential around the NFL.

"I love those guys; they are my boys," Taylor said. "We've grown together…we're like brothers. I don't want to sell myself short to say all my success is due to one source, but they are a part of it, they are my weapon."

Back when Taylor was first discovering PFF, the outside world didn't know much about how NFL contracts worked, and teams were routinely making decisions that we now know are highly inefficient. Fitzgerald and OverTheCap.com changed all that.

"For the longest time when it comes to contracts it was a closed little circle in the NFL," Fitzgerald said.

In 2007, right around the time PFF was starting to gain momentum, Fitzgerald decided that he wanted to look closer into the world of NFL contracts because he was frustrated by the fan dialogue surrounding the New York Jets' front office. When the team won, nobody said a thing, but when they struggled the media and fans would gripe about the team handing out bad contracts. He wanted to see if that was really the case. So Fitzgerald started a website called Jets Cap, where he gathered as much information as he could about the Jets' salary cap, put players' contracts into tables, and started writing about his findings.

Jets beat reporters started to notice that Fitzgerald had accurate information and began to cite his work. When superstar cornerback Darrelle Revis held out of training camp with hopes of a mega contract, Fitzgerald covered it from every angle possible and started seeing his name pop up in the *New York Post* and *Star-Ledger*. Someone from the Jets called Fitzgerald to tell him that he was barking up the right tree.

He expanded after that to covering the salaries of AFC East teams and built out the website to include dead cap figures. That developed into OverTheCap.com, which now houses all 32 teams' contract data. Fitzgerald has contacts around the league who assist in helping him get as close as possible to the correct figures.

Having the data available publicly has changed the way contracts and the salary cap are covered around the league.

"You can't just get away now with a GM coming out and going 'We don't worry about salary cap,' and walk away," Fitzgerald said. "You can challenge them on things, or they can come up with different things they're going to say. It's been good with that because the discourse when it comes to understanding the business side of the NFL has gone way, way, way up the same way the analytics discussion and performance discussion has gone way up, this has gone way up too, and I'm a little part of that so it's kind of cool."

By 2016, Fitzgerald had earned credibility around the league and his site was well known by fans and reporters. He got an invitation to participate in an event that Tulane University was hosting in which students would compete in a mock NFL contract negotiation. He would provide contract data and act as a judge.

The Tulane Pro Football Negotiation was in just its second year when he got the invite. Its first run-through only included students at Tulane, but by year two there were 17 law schools competing in a mock contract negotiation for real NFL players, including Josh Norman, Von Miller, Harrison Smith, and Alshon Jeffery. There were two NFL teams represented in 2016. By 2021, more than 20 teams or agencies participated alongside Fitzgerald to act as judges.

"It's a good opportunity for young people to expand and meet like-minded individuals to get a little bit of an idea about NFL contracts," Fitzgerald said. "You're doing a contract negotiation in 40 minutes or an hour or whatever, that's not realistic, but it's a good way to get into it and understand the metrics and the ways you want to prepare for it. For the students who have gone to that program and been involved with organizing it, it's been really good for them to get a foot in the door in the league in different roles."

Brad Spielberger went to law school at Tulane because he wanted to work in an NFL front office. He had no idea what type of job he wanted in football, but he was fascinated by the chess match NFL teams played every offseason and wanted to be part of that game. One of the first things he learned about within the university's sports law program was the negotiation competition. That's where he met Fitzgerald.

Spielberger asked if he could lend a hand with OverTheCap.com and learn about how NFL contracts work. Fitzgerald gave him the green light and together they wrote a book about draft capital called *The Drafting Stage: Creating a Marketplace for NFL Draft Picks.*

Fitzgerald mentioned to Neil Hornsby that it might be a good idea for PFF to get involved with the Tulane competition. Eric Eager became a judge and PFF came to an agreement to share PFF data with the students who were competing.

Around that same time, PFF and OverTheCap formed an agreement to share data. OTC would let PFF use its contract numbers to study; PFF would give Fitzgerald data that wasn't available to the public, like Eager's Wins Above Replacement stats.

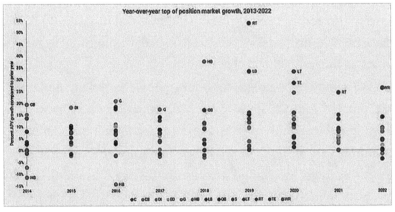

A study by cap expert Brad Spielberger showed changing positional values in the NFL.

With new information came a need to study it. PFF hired Spielberger to analyze contracts and react to the latest deals around the league.

Here is an example from an article in which Spielberger looked at which positions had seen the most growth in average annual salary. He discovered that the receiver market took a huge jump in 2022.

Here's another discovery: suddenly, the NFL began valuing right tackles nearly the same as left tackles, which may have been a reaction to the increase in talented pass-rushers or defenders moving around to both sides of the line.

Spielberger came along at the right time to deep-dive into a changing NFL landscape.

During the rapid acceleration of the NFL's usage of data, there has been a sea change in how much teams focus on positional value. Back in 2012, for example, star running backs Adrian Peterson and Chris Johnson signed megadeals that pretty quickly proved to be inefficient. Their contracts from a decade ago would still be among the highest in 2022, despite the fact that the salary cap has shot up from $120 million to $208 million.

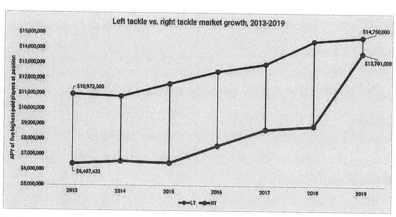

Left and right tackles are now valued similarly in the NFL, when that wasn't always the case.

"There was a change if you look at the contracts; teams kind of got smart to like, 'We can't just let every position market just grow in perpetuity and not recognize that we're not getting good return on investment,'" Spielberger said.

While PFF isn't directly responsible for the NFL figuring out that paying running backs massive dollars was inefficient—analytics pioneers like Aaron Schatz and Brian Burke had been shouting that from the rooftops for years—its work has been part of the larger picture of the league using a data- and research-driven approach with the aim of becoming as shrewd as possible when the margins are razor thin.

"When PFF started to catch on around 2011, a lot of the stuff they did, especially as it pertained to statistics of offensive linemen, defensive linemen, coverage statistics, that was stuff that wasn't being done before," Fitzgerald said. "It's been big in cutting through and seeing what guys fit the system best, what guys make sense, what guys are stat compilers versus actual efficient players, then trying to figure out where they fit on the contract scale to bring those guys in."

Whether teams directly use the PFF data or not in negotiations with players is unclear and probably varies, but we have reached the point where obvious statistical missteps are being avoided in player valuations.

"The old-school metrics on linebackers, you just looked at tackle total," Fitzgerald said. "If this guy is getting 130 tackles, I doubt he's getting them all in the backfield; most of them are probably coming because the defensive line stinks and maybe he's making a couple tackles in the secondary. I think we're looking at the wrong thing."

Now that the league has gotten past paying running backs and tackle-monster linebackers, one development that appears to be on the horizon is teams leaning toward rolling the dice at quarterback rather than locking themselves in long term to their proven QB if he isn't considered elite.

"The Kirk Cousins, Derek Carrs or whatever of the world… can you win with a $50 million-per-year Aaron Rodgers, and what you lose from that? Yes," Spielberger said. "Can you win with a $35 million Kirk Cousins and what you lose from that? No."

Spielberger cites Baker Mayfield as an example. Five to seven years ago, the Browns would have extended Mayfield after a 2021 playoff win against the Pittsburgh Steelers. But instead, Cleveland wanted to wait another year before buying in fully.

"Cleveland, being one of the foremost analytics teams in the NFL, said, 'Look, we need to see him repeat this,'" Spielberger said.

In his study of positional value, Spielberger is finding that all the discussions aren't as straightforward as not paying running backs and middling quarterbacks. PFF WAR has discovered that a safety or cornerback can be worth twice the value of a pass-rusher at their absolute best, but defensive ends are much more consistent from year to year.

"It's looking at how the position markets were and starting to question things and poking holes…teams are asking, 'Why are we paying guys certain amounts?'" Spielberger said.

The impact of more precise player valuations can be seen in the draft. For example, Vikings GM Kwesi Adofo-Mensah traded down from the 12th and 46th picks to acquire the 32nd, 34th, and 66th selections. Under the traditional draft value chart, which was invented by famed Cowboys coach Jimmy Johnson, the Vikings got crushed in the trade. But Spielberger and Fitzgerald's chart is centered on a data-based approach to player value and the possibility of success at each draft slot, rather than Johnson's arbitrary numbers. Harvard created another data-based chart of their own to evaluate trades. The data-driven charts liked the trade for the Vikings.

"Every year they are getting closer and closer to even on the advanced trade charts, and I think that's not a coincidence," Spielberger said.

Valuing contracts and draft picks ties into a bigger-picture aspect of managing teams that has been mastered in the NBA: the timeline.

When the Philadelphia 76ers tore down their entire franchise with the intent of being terrible for several years, calling it "The Process," they showed the world a first-or-last approach that was not generally considered acceptable in the NFL. Some teams (see: the Colts and Suck for Luck) were in position to lose already and happily drafted high and rebuilt their rosters, but now clubs are going out of their way to allow talent to walk to accumulate more draft capital, whether it be from trading good/expensive players away or simply drafting high. Former Miami Dolphins coach Brian Flores even accused owner Stephen Ross of offering to pay him extra to lose games in order to get the No. 1 overall selection. Spielberger uses two recent examples of teams trading their quarterbacks to rebuild rather than putting competitive—but non-contending—teams on the field.

"Seattle with Russell Wilson or Detroit with Matthew Stafford, these quarterbacks might be Hall of Fame quarterbacks—they could have kept them and tried to fix the roster and nail a draft and go 7–9 three years in a row and then maybe figure things out, but for the first time ever teams are saying that being .500 and picking 13th is the worst place you can be in football," Spielberger said. "You want to be in the playoffs, or you want to be the worst team in the NFL to a degree…. Teams are being more realistic with themselves."

Sometimes being realistic can mean the 2021 Los Angeles Rams trading most of their draft capital for an all-in run at the Super Bowl. But Spielberger found that the idea that the Rams' approach to trading away picks is going to catch fire around the league might be dubious. He wrote at PFF.com:

> The conversation needs to be more about surplus value over the contract than just: 'Is X veteran player going to be better than this draft pick?' The real question is: Will they be so much better as to justify losing out on potential surplus value from a stud rookie on a cost-controlled deal? Sometimes they will, but no team should ever count on that being the case. We're not suggesting teams should *never* trade draft capital for veteran players, of course not. But the reality of the situation is that it's as much of a gamble as making a draft selection.

Even with the progress, it still seems like teams (and the football-watching public) are just beginning to see the light when it comes to fully grasping player value and the ins and outs of contracts. Spielberger is going to be right in the center of it.

"He's going to be a huge player in our future," Eager said.

Chapter 19

GOODBYE, NEIL

ONE YEAR AFTER I visited Neil Hornsby's house and sat beside his kidney-shaped pool and chatted for hours about the history of Pro Football Focus, I arrived again in Cincinnati to talk in person about everything that had transpired over the preceding months. I figured that it wouldn't have been right to grill Neil over a Zoom call about stepping away from the company that he had built from a personal computer to an NFL behemoth.

"Do you want to walk and talk?" Neil asked, greeting me at the door along with his three dogs.

"Let's do it."

I didn't realize Neil meant that we were going to walk every step of his entire neighborhood, including strolling through every cul-de-sac and then retracing our steps. He said it was only a couple miles, but my iPhone step counter and severe sunburn had a different opinion. As we wandered by landscapers and dodged the occasional SUV like kids playing in the street, we discussed what life is like for him now and how it got this way.

Neil explained some and vented some.

He felt strongly that the root of PFF's success was collecting, selling, and building products to integrate its data. To Neil, that was PFF's DNA; it was what it was good at doing on a fundamental level. To compete in the media space, in his opinion, PFF would need to dedicate a much greater percentage of the Silver Lake investment money to that side of the business than it was able and would need even more money and people with more experience building a consumer business than it already had. But Cris Collinsworth saw the matter differently, believing that they could succeed with just the $10 million allotted to that side and his son Austin and George Chahrouri leading the charge.

"You cannot have a CEO who doesn't believe in the strategy of the business," Neil said.

If the investment money weren't a factor, maybe the two sides could have coexisted and slowly made progress. But Silver Lake's investment brought along pressure to take PFF from a 160-million-dollar company to a billion-dollar company. Neil thought that they could get there by focusing on the consumer side, but they would have to take an all-in approach in an extremely crowded space where other football media outlets already have a foothold that would require more money—lots more, in Neil's opinion.

"We've had the best football data on the planet for 15 years and so far, we've built at best adequate consumer products," Neil said. "Our gambling algorithms are fine, but the nature of the space, with small sample sizes of games, means you can be beaten many times by guys in Vegas smoking cigars, wearing lots of rings, and pulling predictions out of their ass. It's not like B2B, where a key opinion-maker looks at what you've built, understands its value, and sends you a check every year. Consumer at this level is more of a marketing game, and marketing is about money. If you want to win, you need to persuade people who have never heard of you before to buy your product, not your million Twitter followers."

Neil was not a believer in the idea that more average football fans would seek PFF out en masse to make enough money to satisfy Silver Lake. After all, the PFF consumer brand had long operated by attracting a particular type of fan—one who was extremely curious about the game behind the game. Neil wondered, *Would Joe Fan who watches the game on Sunday and then goes to mow his lawn and mostly doesn't think about the NFL until the following Sunday really engage with our consumer products?* Jazz is more complicated musically than rock, but more people listen to rock. PFF has 1 million Twitter followers. ESPN has 46 million.

"There is another way to do this more slowly and thoughtfully, but you need someone in charge who has done this before," Neil said. "With only $10 million, you have zero room for error."

Eventually they agreed that nothing was going to change and reached an impasse. Neil understood that, back in 2014, he had sold Collinsworth the right to take PFF whatever direction he chose, which meant that Neil was the one who had to step away.

Every time Neil wanted to emphasize a point, we would stop walking. It occurred to me that his neighbors might have thought we were having an argument. He came to a complete halt to explain that if he felt confident in who was running the consumer business, he would be able to accept moving away from his life's work. But losing Austin Gayle to The Ringer shook him. He felt something more was wrong than a disagreement over how to spend money.

"When you start losing people like Austin…it becomes every single thing that we didn't value in PFF, virtually all the stuff that we didn't agree with, is now becoming manifest," Hornsby said. "That's hard for me to swallow."

Neil says that he hopes he's wrong. He jokes that he is rooting to be an old man shouting at clouds, no matter how strongly he believes that they should have gone another direction with PFF.

"You might think I'm sitting on the sidelines saying, 'Please fail!' But that's my baby," Hornsby said. "I want to be wrong."

Neil worries that PFF won't know how to connect products with sales in the consumer market. He worries that the core beliefs that PFF was built on will fade. He didn't say it out loud, but he might be most worried about the Originals, whom he kept intact from day one through the present. All Neil can do now is worry.

"I felt like we were this close, we were 95 percent of the way to having a great, enduring business, and it was like the finish line was just there but it felt like it was snatched away," Neil said. "We had well over $10 million in the bank before Silver Lake ever came along. That money should have been used to pay our people world-class salaries, give them an LTIP [long term incentive plan], and get them ready for an assault on the peak. $1 billion was always my goal too; I just saw a different way of achieving it."

Inside the walls of PFF, people who are connected enough to know what has been going on are split. Some feel that Neil made things chaotic and that settling on a defined direction will set them free. Others are skeptical of inexperienced management taking on a monumental task.

It's ironic in some ways, because Collinsworth was deeply concerned that taking the investment money from Silver Lake would change things—and it did, almost instantly, just not in the way that he anticipated. Nobody anticipated it would ultimately lead to Neil's exit.

"A lot of people have asked me the question: If you knew what you know now, would you have still sold the company to Cris Collinsworth, knowing that you'd take the company that you founded off in this direction?" Neil said. "My answer would be: 100 times out of 100, yes, I would have done the same thing. We've been able to create jobs. We've been able to work with teams. We've been able to follow our passion, we've seen people grow…it's been a hell of a ride. It's just been as fun as it possibly could be."

On June 30, 2022, Neil announced his retirement. The unfortunate part is that if he had gone along with Collinsworth's path, he probably would have worked as PFF's CEO for a few more years and then walked away. Had he done that, PFF's employees would have lined up along the streets outside of the PFF offices to give him an ovation as he left the building for the final time.

Instead, he went without much fanfare. He had a goodbye party in late August. Lots of longtime PFFers showed up. Eric Eager noticeably did not. That hurt Neil. Khaled Elsayed, Ben Stockwell, Jon Berger, and Peter King sent video messages congratulating him on his career with PFF. Steve Palazzolo did the voiceover for a video the team produced about the history of PFF.

"We always expected that there would be a ride off into the sunset for Neil," Palazzolo said. "I thought it would be a little more glamorous. It's a little sad because…everybody owes some sort of debt of gratitude to Neil, but there's eight or 10 of us that really do."

Despite his company's profound impact on the NFL, there were no tweets from ESPN's Adam Schefter or a segment on NFL Network dedicated to the man who put an incalculable amount of data in the hands of all 32 teams and helped drive the league's analytics revolution—a man whose company was responsible for the Eagles' Super Bowl–winning touchdowns and only god knows how many other game plans and coaches', executives', and data scientists' careers. Jon Berger, the Giants director of football information who first found PFF, agreed with the idea that Neil belongs in the Pro Football Hall of Fame as a contributor.

Here's what Neil sent to everyone at PFF to announce he was leaving:

In some of the less surprising news of the year, I'd like to announce I'll be leaving PFF to begin the next chapter of my story.

For the last 15 years, I've put PFF ahead of everything in my life, including (perhaps to my shame) my immediate family. I didn't do so in order to build the biggest business or to make the most money or to achieve any type of personal fame. I did so out of loyalty to the people who, right from the start, decided to give this crazy "hobby" of mine a chance and also, to paraphrase my good friend Austin Gayle, "I guess I just loved being part of a winning team". I know there are so many other people at PFF who have made similar sacrifices for the same reasons.

All the best times I have had at PFF came from collective endeavor and the joy of shared success:

- Mine and Khaled's childlike astonishment as our initial process of inputting games for analysis turned from an hour-a-game slog to a button push per week thanks to Ian Perks' brilliance and then five years later, seeing K and Geoff Lane turn that process into the D.A.T.

- Ian and I sitting in my living room in Luton watching the first consumer sale register in the system and then ten years later me texting back and forth with Austin, as another daily budget was beaten, and another record smashed.

- In 2012, Bryan Hall and I begging for meetings at the combine, getting one with the Panthers and being told recently by one of the customers from that meeting, Rob Rogers (now with the Commanders), he knew "...the moment that Bryan opened his laptop that football had changed forever."

- A week after scribbling something unintelligible on a white board seeing Brad Condo make it come to life and then watching as Rick Drummond, Alex Padgett & Kenny Glenn took it on and made PFF ULTI-MATE the preeminent tool in football. Then, years later, having Steve Palazzolo pitch, on EXACTLY that same whiteboard, the concept of PFF IQ.

- And, in perhaps the most cyclical of these vignettes, ten years after I had specified and Ian had coded a 30+ page scouting report that was meant as nothing other than a demonstration of how the data could be used, finding out that last year, my son Ben, had to rewrite the whole thing to access the new database, as many NFL teams were still using it.

Looking back now it's hard to conceive of how so many people would give so much of themselves for so little obvious reward. To those from the early days I've already mentioned above, add the names of Ben Stockwell, Sam Monson, Nathan Jahnke and Mike Parker. By way of example, Mike gave up a job with XOS and worked his first nine months at PFF, for literally nothing, on the busi-ness-critical task of linking our data to video. Why would anyone do that? Why did you do it Mike? I'm guessing for the same reasons I mentioned earlier. It was an opportu-nity to spend time with other wonderful, talented, selfless people in a meritocracy, based on shared values. A team that nearly always led the market with unique data and ideas taking precedence over a lust for money. One mantra running through every person and everything—Under Promise, Over DELIVER!

When Cris purchased the company in 2014, I felt the same sense of loyalty to him as I did to the rest of the team—I had an obsessive desire to ensure his investment didn't die on the vine whilst never wanting to lose sight of the values that were the bedrock of our initial success. Clearly, the investment paid off and I hope I never betrayed my core beliefs in helping achieve that. Last year the company was valued at almost 30 times what Cris and Jack Cassidy initially paid.

My proudest moment from this period was that during Co-Vid [sic], nobody lost their job as a result of the pandemic, no one took a pay cut, we never took a cent of government handout and when I asked Cris if he was OK with the financial implications his response was "sure .... we'll just make less money this year" and in saying that confirmed for both of us at least, good businesses don't have to be purely about the bottom line. The very next year we smashed every budget we'd set, and everyone shared in that success with a bigger than advertised bonus. Everyone loves to leave on a high and 2021 was, in that regard, a wonderful way to sign off.

When Dan Marino retired in 1999, I realized I wasn't really a Dolphins fan, I was a Dan Marino fan.

As I retire from PFF, I realize I'm not so much a PFF fan as I am of the people who worked so diligently to make it what it became. Those for whom it was never about them, didn't ask for anything they hadn't earned and who only wanted to be part of a winning team. There are no words I could come up with to adequately convey my gratitude to you all.

I wish you all the very best going forward and hope you will say in touch. I will miss you more than you will ever know.

Before we walked back inside to cool off and eat popsicles by his backyard construction site, I asked Neil about that legacy and the fact that he will go underappreciated by the outside world because he didn't self-promote on social media or evangelize analytics in the public eye.

"I'm the luckiest bastard," Neil said. "I feel like the luckiest person on the planet."

Neil doesn't care about how he's viewed by anyone except his PFF colleagues, NFL customers, and people inside the game like Fred Gaudelli. He wants to have their admiration and that's it. He always told employees that Collinsworth and the data were the stars of the company, not him or anyone else.

Neil allowed me to write about PFF because I wanted to do it, not because he wanted someone to write about him. He didn't ask to read the book before it was published. He didn't demand that anything be left uncovered. From day one, Neil said, "Tell the whole story, good and bad."

Before I leave, Claire asks if I want some aloe for my sunburn, which has turned full lobster-red. We talk at dinner about the crazy year-plus from my first arrival in Cincinnati and all the things that happened within the walls of PFF in a short time. It's especially weird for Neil that, for the first time since he picked up *Touchdown* magazine at a train station in Liverpool, he won't be obsessively focused on NFL data.

Neil said he's going to keep the first check from an NFL team in his office and the picture of Austin Gayle and his brother that Austin gave to him one day and that has been on his office desk ever since. The TVs will stay in his office so he can watch all the college football games at once, even if he's not DVRing them to put in the PFF system anymore. And the many people whose careers he sparked will stop by to watch.

"The friendships will definitely last forever," Neil said before I grabbed an Uber to head to the airport.

In the months after Neil and I walked around the Cincy suburbs talking about his retirement, multiple PFFers told me that they were trying to get Neil to help them with the problems inside the company. Current employees were telling Neil about the culture inside the building taking a nosedive. They were telling him the numbers weren't matching Silver Lake's expectations, and folks on the consumer side were worried that their ability to deliver to teams was going to be affected if things didn't get turned around.

In October 2022, Neil called me, and he was upset. We talked for two hours about everything that was going on and how he wasn't sleeping well because of the stress, which was palpable over the phone. Those working for PFF have always looked to Neil as their leader through thick and thin—and they didn't know who else to turn to in order to get Collinsworth's attention. So Neil gathered their comments and put them into a long letter to Collinsworth asking him to make a change in leadership because he was concerned that the people whose career dreams PFF made true were going to either leave in the same way that Austin Gayle and Eric Eager had or be deeply unhappy with their jobs. He read the letter to me over the phone with agony in his voice. While he didn't want it published, the overall message to Collinsworth was, "You have to do something." It wasn't about the financial stuff; it was about the people he cared for within those walls.

Not long after sending his note to Collinsworth, Neil was scheduled to have heart surgery. The stress from his impending surgery combined with everything at PFF had him tied up in knots. He kindly sent a note to his friends at PFF asking them to avoid sharing PFF's internal happenings while he recovered. Talk football, talk family, but the state of the company was keeping him awake too many nights.

Before we hung up, I told Neil it was time to put a wrap on my PFF reporting. But I asked one more question: *Are you going to end up back at PFF by the time this thing comes out?*

He laughed.

"That would be good for the book, wouldn't it?"

EPILOGUE

A FTER SPENDING A YEAR reporting on the history of Pro Football Focus and talking extensively with the people who made it the most influential data company in football, one particular conversation stands out in my memory. Before diving into our interview, Rick Drummond asked, "Why are you writing this book now when our story isn't written and we still have a long way to go?" My response was that all history books are out of date by the time they are published. That is the case when it comes to technology and data companies. The landscape changes fast. I had to pick an end date for my reporting; otherwise it would go on and on forever. So it's very possible that things have already changed significantly within PFF by the time you're reading this. Consider this a snapshot of the moment when football underwent a tectonic shift in its belief in technology and PFF was standing there ready for the data revolution. Mike Parker told me that if Neil Hornsby had come along 10 years earlier, nobody would have taken him seriously, and if he'd come along 10 years later, he would have been too late.

The timing of PFF's rise isn't interesting just because it was Johnny on the Spot when the NFL was finally ready to make some of the same advancements that had previously only been seen in baseball and basketball. It also came at a time in which sports fans were becoming increasingly knowledgeable about and intrigued by the idea of hidden truths in sports. Across the globe, Neil found people who were similarly fascinated by the concept of the football coaches and broadcasters on TV not always having all the answers. What if the Pro Bowl selections weren't always right? What if they shouldn't punt on fourth-and-1? What if football could be analyzed deeper and done smarter? Neil found people who were driven by the idea that they could be trailblazing new paths in football the same way many in the baseball analytics space had done before them. If Neil came along 10 years earlier, the Rick Drummonds and Steve Palazzolos wouldn't have known what analytics were. If he'd come along 10 years later, nobody would have felt like they were blazing trails and working for purpose rather than pay.

I also thought a great deal about whether Neil will ever get the credit he deserves within the community of people who control football narratives. Inside the NFL, many consider him a Hall of Fame–worthy contributor, but the outside world's understanding of how Neil and PFF have impacted the NFL is limited. During the writing process, I noticed one major media outlet NFL reporter tweet that they have never taken anything PFF does seriously. I guess they never asked what PFF does. And many reporters and commentators don't want to know, because they spent far too many keystrokes on all the things the grading system couldn't tell you. A simple Google search reveals dozens of reporters' appeals to authority with headlines like "Coach says to take PFF grades with a grain of salt," despite the fact the authority figures in the NFL were implementing PFF's data behind the scenes and using it to win the Super Bowl. Had Neil been a Bill James–like personality—had he tweeted more or given TED talks or urged reporters to profile him repeatedly—maybe he would have gotten more acknowledgement along the way. Instead, the *Cincinnati Business Courier* was the only publication that wrote about his retirement. But that's not what Neil wanted. He wanted for his customers—football teams—to like his product and love working with his company. That's it. You won't find too many folks like that in the 2020s.

With Neil gone from PFF, the company will navigate a space that is only growing more crowded by the day. There aren't just other football-obsessed people like Neil who are spending endless hours trying to develop the next great analytical invention; there are companies with gargantuan budgets that have realized the ground for data sales might be fertile in the age of analytics in sports. Someday someone will come up with a product that aims to take NFL and college teams away from PFF. When Neil was in charge, the way they kept the data geniuses on the outside away was through the relationships that Neil and his team built. They could tailor their product to teams' specifications because they knew everyone and got tons of feedback. Will PFF's human touch matter as much as they go into the future? Will it remain as strong without a person in charge who prioritized those relationships over everything else?

And it feels like we are only at the beginning of football's acceptance of analytics. Most teams only have a couple of people, at most, breaking down the numbers. The New York Yankees reportedly have more than 20 analysts. NFL teams are bound to close that gap soon, particularly with NextGEN digital tracking data just starting to catch on. Can PFF continue to grow alongside a generation of new GMs like Kwesi Adofo-Mensh, who have degrees in things like economics and finance rather than the sidelines and trenches?

Some of the same questions could be asked about PFF's role in leading the discussion. In the same way that Baseball Prospectus lived at the top of the baseball data movement in the public eye for years and then saw dozens of other sites pop up and the major media companies like ESPN and MLB Network start covering baseball statistics, PFF too faces the potential for others to track it down in the public innovation realm. That's partly because of the sheer number of people trying to say something new about America's favorite game, but also because PFF could become a stepping stone for promising football minds like Austin Gayle, who left for The Ringer, rather than a lifetime career like it has been for Steve Palazzolo and Sam Monson.

Work environments change too. After COVID, people have been much more apt to leave jobs in search of something better. It even coined a new term: The Great Resignation. That didn't apply very much to PFF in its existence through 2022, but the company isn't immune to it. In order to succeed in the early days, PFF built a competitive environment where the Mike Renners and Austin Gayles grinded their way into prominent front-facing roles. As the company gets bigger, will that path still exist, or will PFF spend its investment dollars to bring in outside media talent and take away the carrot that drove those who were trying to gain an edge?

There are other considerations facing PFF, like how an expanding fantasy and gambling market could make it a wild success or leave it sucking the dust of more established brands. Will the subscription bubble eventually burst? With everyone from Disney to the smallest newspaper asking for x dollars per month, is there a breaking point where people aren't as willing to add on one more thing?

And how much longer will Cris Collinsworth be the face of the company and its guiding hand? He turned 63 in January 2022 and is still taking on a hefty broadcasting load.

Every company that grows up faces similar questions. The infrastructure in place gives PFF every opportunity to remain football's Chosen Data Company and the thinking football fan's place to go to understand the game better. But the question is whether PFF can find a way to replicate the same thrill that Nathan had in creating spreadsheets with player equipment in order to master player participation or that Neil had after getting his first call from an NFL team.

I tend to think so. Football is for passionate and competitive people. Sometimes they look like Zac Robinson, sometimes they look like Tej Seth, but they are cut from the same cloth. PFF will thrive so long as it continues to be built on the shoulders of those looking for a dream job in football the same way the Originals once did. Plus, football always presents new problems that need to be solved, and PFF will be there looking for answers so long as the company follows Collinsworth's advice: "Don't ever get to the point where you say, 'We cracked the code.'"